LET BEAUTY SPEAK

Jimmy Mitchell

LET BEAUTY SPEAK

*The Art of Being Human
in a Culture of Noise*

IGNATIUS PRESS   SAN FRANCISCO

Nihil Obstat: Very Reverend Joseph L. Waters
                 Censor Librorum

Imprimatur: +The Most Reverend Gregory L. Parkes
               Bishop of St. Petersburg
               February 15, 2022

Cover photo by Béatrice Prève

Cover design by Jimmy Mitchell and John Herreid

© 2023 by Ignatius Press, San Francisco
All rights reserved
ISBN 978-1-62164-606-8 (PB)
ISBN 978-1-64229-258-9 (eBook)
Library of Congress Control Number 2022941285
Printed in the United States of America ∞

For Pope Benedict XVI,
whose life and writings have forever shaped my own.

*Who knows whether you have not come to the kingdom
for such a time as this?*

—Esther 4:14

CONTENTS

FOREWORD

One of my intellectual heroes once told me that "nostalgia makes a poor excuse for tradition". Too many people yearn for a golden age of the distant past without ever seeking to make the age they live in better. It seems to me that the more uncertain the age, the stronger the yearning to go back. I sense this in myself, in the company I keep, and in the students whom I have had the privilege to teach. But we cannot go back, nor should we. For if we did, we would likely bring the illnesses of our age with us. Rather, we ought to bring forward what is good, true, and beautiful in every age and ensure it is deeply rooted in our own. The temptation of uncertain times—and we do live in uncertain times—is to run either from the future or from our past. We set up edifices, draw lines in the sand, create new vocabulary to describe our camp, but the resulting tribalism does nothing to advance the Gospel, renew culture, or serve the common good. We may be broken people in a broken world, but we are pilgrims, not fugitives. We are not meant to run away, rather to journey toward.

The task of every generation is to face its challenges with courage and vigor and receive its blessings with humility and gratitude. Our post-Christian culture will not be evangelized by a program or a campaign, but by the individual witness of lives lived well—on fire with genuine joy and hope and a fierce determination that we are made for something more than this current world has to offer. In other words, if we are to renew our culture, we must first renew ourselves. To do this well, four things are needed. First, we must have a deep sense of who we are and what we are made for—an identity rooted in our being unique, unrepeatable, beloved sons and daughters of God the Father. Second, we must seek out and cultivate real community—the type whose diversity strengthens and hones, whose charity serves and perfects. Third, we must have a deep sense of urgency to share the good news and joyfully witness to what God has done in our own lives—an authentic and personal proclamation of the kerygma. Lastly, we must cooperate with God's life-giving grace—a participative *fiat* to God's invitation to do the work that he has called us to do.

Forsaking one's heritage is loathsome. So too is ignoring one's vocation to the time and place in which God has set one. It is a form of high arrogance to think that you would have been better off, more virtuous, or holier if you were born forty, fifty, or five hundred years ago. For reasons known to God alone, you are here in this time and in this place, with all its challenges and all its opportunities. *How will you respond?*

This short book will help you answer this question with greater clarity and a renewed sense of joy and hope. Now, more than ever, we need to let beauty speak and rediscover the art of being human in a world desperate for meaning and truth.

Ryan Hanning, Ph.D.
Feast of the Nativity of Saint John the Baptist, 2022
White's Creek, Tennessee

INTRODUCTION

It's tempting to exaggerate the novelty of our age. Every generation tends to think that its struggles are unique or worse than those of the generations preceding them. While the last couple of years have been confounding and at times chaotic, the existential threats we face today are the same as those faced by every great generation in human history. Think of the fall of the Roman Empire, the Great Schism of 1054, the Reformation, or the two great World Wars of the last century. Major crises have a way of fundamentally reshaping culture while accentuating the perennial questions found in every human heart: *What does it mean to be human? How do I live my faith amid hostility and division? What's my unique and unrepeatable role to play at this moment in history?*

Personal tragedy or global disaster is often what it takes to slow us down long enough to confront reality and ask where our lives are going, what our lives are about, and how we can make a difference in the world. Because we live in a culture dominated by relativism, it's rare for people to ask these philosophical questions. Relativism has overshadowed the pursuit of truth and goodness, convincing us that it's intolerant to propose anything absolute. In today's world, any disagreement with mainstream media or higher education is a thought crime. Traditional morality is considered bigoted and out of step with the times.

This relativism has led to a culture of noise that fills our everyday lives with endless distractions. Most of us scroll

our phones long enough every year to cover the distance
to the top of Mount Everest and back.[1] Technology and
media have become the new arbiters of truth and purvey-
ors of culture. In the words of Robert Cardinal Sarah, our
society "stubbornly hates silence" and all that comes with
it.[2] The noise is pervasive, and the vestiges of Christian
values are few and far between.

While there are pockets of holiness everywhere, the
West has become increasingly hostile to the faith com-
pared to the past. Think back to the Catholic villages of
France in the height of the Middle Ages, where every
church bell rang at noon as a reminder to pray the Angelus. Think back to a time when the pope was the great
patron of the arts, commissioning masterpieces by everyone from Michelangelo to Mozart. Think back to 1950s
America when Catholic bishop Fulton J. Sheen won an
Emmy Award for his weekly show on prime-time television. The past wasn't perfect, but the Church has been
losing ground in the West for decades. Over the last few
years, the implosion of Christian faith and culture has
accelerated at a rapid pace with the relegation of religion
outside of the public square.

Meanwhile, our hearts are filled with quiet desperation.
The noise has numbed our infinite desire for God, and
our culture is sinking into despair. Yet, the Lord is calling
the Church to step into the gap and remind the world
what it means to be human. How can we propose a *way of
life* that transcends historical eras and evangelizes others by
first inspiring them to live their humanity well?

---

[1] "Average Person Scrolls Height of Everest in a Year—Measure Your
Thumb Mileage Here", *Irish Examiner*, May 30, 2018, www.irishexaminer
.com/lifestyle/arid-30845961.html.

[2] Robert Cardinal Sarah, *The Power of Silence against the Dictatorship of Noise*,
trans. Michael J. Miller (San Francisco: Ignatius Press, 2017), p. 56.

Throughout most of my college years, I thought being a Christian was about living a morally upright life and winning theological debates whenever possible. I argued with friends in coffee shops and did whatever it took to convince them that I was right and they were wrong. I often tried to win them over with charm and persuasion, but I quickly turned them into intellectual projects and hijacked their dignity (while losing something of my own) along the way. After several years as a frustrated evangelist, I began praying and fasting. I studied history and philosophy. I looked to the lives of great saints and reformers to see how they won souls and spearheaded entire movements of renewal in the life of the Church.

Over the course of several months, a consistent pattern became evident: great evangelists never took their eyes off beauty. They fixed their gaze constantly upon the Beautiful One who gave them their identity every day in prayer. They surrendered constantly to Divine Providence and allowed God to orchestrate their lives into a beautiful masterpiece. Their relationship with Jesus Christ wasn't a transaction but a romance. They found him in the beauty of creation as effortlessly as they revealed him through the beauty of their lives. They believed deeply that adhering to a divine ideal was the only route to personal renewal, which would in turn lead to cultural renewal. They let the beauty of God's love speak to the deepest recesses of their hearts, and the beauty of their holiness evangelized the world around them.

While there are many enemies of truth and goodness in today's culture of noise, rare are the enemies of beauty. Very few argue with a blood-orange sunset, a towering mountain range, a newborn child, or an ancient church. Above all, nobody argues with the beauty of the saints— from the humble witness of Mother Teresa to the joyful wit of G.K. Chesterton. The saints have always been the greatest apologetic of every age. When beauty speaks through their holiness, it cuts through all the noise and brings truth and goodness along with it. These words from the early Christian theologian Tertullian demonstrate this truth as he mocks the enemies of the early Church:

> But do your worst, and rack your inventions for tortures for Christians—it is all to no purpose; you do but attract the world, and make it fall the more in love with our religion; the more you mow us down, the thicker we rise; the Christian blood you spill is like the seed you sow, it springs from the earth again, and fructifies the more.[3]

Is there anything more powerful than Christians who are fearless before the prospect of death? In the words of Tertullian, their witness will only make others "fall the more in love" with Christ and his Church. In fact, the early Church grew by 40 percent a decade in spite of endless persecutions.[4] It's only when the Church gets comfortable that she turns in on herself, fades in her beauty, and begins contracting in size.

What role, then, does beauty play in breaking through the noise, cultivating our humanity, and evangelizing our culture? There are countless ways of looking at beauty, most of them beyond the scope of this book. In brief, Plato argues that beauty is not a mere attraction in the eye of the beholder but an *objective reality* in what is

---

[3] Tertullian, *Apologeticus Adversus Gentes Pro Christianis*, ed. T. Herbert Bindley (Oxford: Clarendon Press, 1889), p. 143.

[4] Rodney Stark, *The Rise of Christianity: How the Obscure, Marginal Jesus Movement Became the Dominant Religious Force in the Western World in a Few Centuries* (Princeton, NJ: Princeton University Press, 1996), p. 3.

beheld.[5] According to Saint Thomas Aquinas, "Beauty relates to the cognitive faculty; for beautiful things are those which please when seen."[6] Swiss theologian Hans Urs von Balthasar calls beauty the "word which shall be our first" as he explains its inseparable relationship with truth and goodness:

> Beauty demands for itself at least as much courage and decision as do truth and goodness, and she will not allow herself to be separated and banned from her two sisters without taking them along with herself in an act of mysterious vengeance. We can be sure that whoever sneers at her name, as if she were the ornament of a bourgeois past, whether he admits it or not, can no longer pray and soon will no longer be able to love.[7]

American theologian John-Mark Miravalle describes beauty as that which "ignites in us ... the desire for what is good and true" and "makes us *long for* higher things, which motivates us to *pursue* higher things, which leads to our ultimate fulfillment".[8] All these explanations lead to the very simple conclusion that beauty points to the divine. Every encounter with beauty is a foretaste of heaven. In his 2002 message to the Communion and Liberation

[5] *Stanford Encyclopedia of Philosophy*, comp. Crispin Sartwell (Summer 2022), s.v. "Beauty", under "Objectivity and Subjectivity", last modified March 2022, https://plato.stanford.edu/entries/beauty/#ObjSub.

[6] Thomas Aquinas, *Summa Theologiae* I, q. 5, art. 4, from *The Summa Theologiæ of St. Thomas Aquinas*, 2nd and rev. ed., trans. Fathers of the English Dominican Province, 1920, New Advent, online ed. by Kevin Knight, 2017. All translations of the *Summa Theologiae* are from this source.

[7] Hans Urs von Balthasar, *The Glory of the Lord: A Theological Aesthetics* (Edinburgh: T&T Clark, 1982), p. 18.

[8] John-Mark L. Miravalle, *Beauty: What It Is and Why It Matters* (Manchester, NH: Sophia Institute Press, 2019), p. 13 (emphasis in original).

movement as prefect of the Congregation for the Doctrine of the Faith, three years before he was elected Pope Benedict XVI, Joseph Cardinal Ratzinger sums it up:

> Is there anyone who does not know Dostoyevsky's often quoted sentence: "The Beautiful will save us"? However, people usually forget that Dostoyevsky is referring here to the redeeming Beauty of Christ. We must learn to see Him. If we know Him, not only in words, but if we are struck by the arrow of his paradoxical beauty, then we will truly know him, and know him not only because we have heard others speak about him. Then we will have found the beauty of Truth, of the Truth that redeems. Nothing can bring us into close contact with the beauty of Christ himself other than the world of beauty created by faith and light that shines out from the faces of the saints, through whom his own light becomes visible.[9]

What is more powerful than Christian culture celebrating the beauty created by faith? What is more captivating than the light of Christ shining out from great music, timeless art, and the faces of the saints? The reevangelization of the West depends on it. With the help of the Holy Spirit, the mobilization of the Church as an instrument of renewal depends on it as well. While beautiful music, art, and architecture all carry great evangelical power, what we need most are heroic Christians living the fullness of the faith and captivating others with the beauty of their holiness. We need the next generation of saints to rise up and evangelize our culture of noise through their distinctly Christian way of life.

[9] Congregation for the Doctrine of the Faith, *Message of His Eminence Card. Joseph Ratzinger to the Communion and Liberation (CL) Meeting at Rimini (24–30 August 2002)*, http://www.vatican.va/roman_curia/congregations/cfaith/docu ments/rc_con_cfaith_doc_20020824_ratzinger-cl-rimini_en.html.

Many books have been published that propose ways to rebuild Christian culture in light of our present situation. What makes *Let Beauty Speak* different? You have in your hands the battle cry of every Christian who seeks to be fully human and fully alive, who wants to engage and redeem the world rather than run away from it. This approach to evangelization is less about techniques and more about lifestyle. It's an art, not a science, inspiring you to live your humanity so well that you can't help but point others to the divine.

This book will teach you how to recognize beauty as an instrument in your own deepening conversion and a tool for evangelizing others. As you apply its principles to your daily life, beauty will inspire you to become more fully human, increasing the joy of your discipleship with Christ and the fruitfulness of your apostolate with him. Over time, beauty will help integrate your faith into your personality, allowing your work of evangelization to be organic rather than forced. Beauty will also inspire a posture of humility, reminding you that Christianity is not a do-it-yourself spirituality but rather a religion of total abandonment.

The last fifteen years of prayer, study, and travel have led me to write this book. Its principles have guided my life for almost as long and informed the lifestyles of countless people I've met along the way. They previously provided the foundation for a year-long formation program for young adults in Nashville; they also inspired a multiweek retreat series livestreamed during the initial outbreak of the coronavirus. They now provide the foundation for Love Good Academy, an ongoing formation platform for Christians committed to evangelizing the world through beauty.

This is not an academic book but rather a how-to guide for living a more human, beautiful, and evangelical way of life. Each chapter is dedicated to a principle and builds on previous chapters, intending to whet your appetite and leave you hungry for more. As I simplify and personalize big ideas throughout the book, I conclude each chapter with practical resolutions and book recommendations that will take you deeper. Since entire libraries have been written on each of these principles, consider this a springboard. Whether these principles are brand new to you or deeply intuitive, this book will give you language, clarity, and courage to invite others into the art of being human. If you can, read through each principle as a small group of friends or as a family. Take notes and keep a journal along the way.

If we can get these ten principles right, we stand a chance at evangelizing our culture of noise. They capture the spirit and grit of countless saints who have gone before us. From embracing childlike wonder to integrating prayer, work, and leisure into our everyday lives, these principles will inspire us to live intentionally and evangelize boldly. They're a wake-up call to transform the world through the beauty of holiness. Together, we must let the beauty of God's love speak to every corner of our hearts so that human history marks our era less by crisis and more by great saints rising up from the ashes. As we turn these principles into a way of life, we'll join the long line of saints whose holiness was the remedy for the isolation, confusion, and meaninglessness of their times.

Jimmy Mitchell
Feast of the Exaltation of the Cross, 2022
Palm Harbor, Florida

Chapter 1

Wonder

'wɔndər | noun | *a feeling of surprise mingled with admiration, caused by something beautiful, unexpected, unfamiliar, or inexplicable.*

One of the greatest adventures of my life began on a plane destined for the Southern Hemisphere. It was January 2016, and I was leaving my Tennessee winter behind for a beautiful New Zealand summer where I'd soon be climbing into hobbit holes and leading a week-long camp for a few hundred teenagers.

Long before I landed in Auckland (the largest city in New Zealand), my sense of wonder was in high gear. On the first flight from my hometown of Nashville to Los Angeles, I looked out my window at dinnertime as we were chasing the sunset. Everywhere I turned, I saw piercing yellows and reds. Because we were traveling west at just the right time of the day, I was experiencing the longest sunset of my life. Later in the flight, I noticed a Nashville Dominican sister in full habit sitting a few rows ahead of me, and I learned that she was an Aussie headed back home after the holidays. She was young and beautiful, and she had a profound joy that immediately made me feel at home. At this point, nothing about my trip to the end of the world felt ordinary.

After the stop in Los Angeles, as we crossed into the Southern Hemisphere and then over the International Date Line, my heart was full of anticipation. It was the farthest I had ever traveled by myself. That would normally be a cause for anxiety, but between the sunset, the religious sister, and my growing sense of wonder, all my nervous energy turned into a readiness for God to do something incredible. I was full of joyful expectancy.

After traveling twenty-four hours, I landed safely in Auckland and immediately hopped on a bus for Hamilton, where I spent the night on a hundred-acre dairy farm. My host was a farmer, and his radical hospitality furthered my forgetfulness about being thousands of miles away from home. After my last bite of fresh eggs and toast the following morning, he handed me off to another friend, who was a couple of years into seminary and easily one of the most joyful, sincere people I'd ever met. Glad for a day off from working on his own family's dairy farm, he led me to his beat-up car with a huge smile on his face and began a day-long tour of the countryside.

We spent well over an hour praying at a local church before disappearing to Hobbiton, a tourist trap ignored by most Kiwis (the word used to describe New Zealanders) and frequented by foreigners. There was a profound joy in being surrounded by fellow Tolkien devotees as I stepped onto the set where Sir Peter Jackson filmed *The Lord of the Rings* and *The Hobbit* trilogies. I ducked inside perfectly preserved hobbit holes and even enjoyed a pint of local beer at the Prancing Pony toward the end of the tour. Again, I felt at home. You can imagine the thrill, the awe, the wonder of it all. I couldn't help but give thanks to God, who was not only present in the beauty of his creation but also in the creative genius of Tolkien, Jackson, and others. In that moment, these words from the

Old Testament were coming to life: "For from the greatness and beauty of created things comes a corresponding perception of their Creator" (Wis 13:5).

The next week unfolded with unforgettable rugby matches, volcano hikes, haka dances, and the profound joy of watching young Kiwis transformed by the love of God. As I jumped into mud pits by day and proclaimed the Gospel by night, I was humbly aware that I still had so much to learn about God, myself, and the world. My own existential questions rose to the surface: *What was my life all about? Where was it going? Why was God continuing to call me on mission—even to the ends of the earth—when I felt so unworthy?*

I have since returned to New Zealand three times and remain grateful beyond words for my sweet memories and beautiful friends. Each successive trip has renewed my sense of wonder and inspired me to ask big questions about life's meaning and my own purpose. At the end of the day, this small country captivates me with its epic sights and endless adventures as much as it inspires me with its creative minority living their Christian faith against the odds.

THE BIG QUESTIONS

When was the last time you stood in awe and wonder? It doesn't have to involve an adventure to another hemisphere. Even in your most ordinary of circumstances, when has beauty led you into an encounter with the living God? When was the last time beauty helped you ask important questions about life's origin, purpose, and final end?

While New Zealand provided me with an unexpected opportunity to cultivate wonder and ask big questions, I can think of many simpler (and far less exotic) moments that similarly changed my life. For example, I'll never forget walking into my first fraternity house as a new freshman at Vanderbilt University. Within five minutes, I had a beer in each hand and a decision to make: *What kind of person did I want to be?* Only a few hours beforehand, my psychology professor had taught me that college was the most formative season of my entire life. If that was true, who I became in those four years was decisive. Moments later, I walked out of that frat house and met a fast friend. He was a talkative Baptist who didn't need alcohol for a good time. There was something striking about how he interacted with others. He was joyful and authentic. Because of his witness, I couldn't help but wonder if there was more to college than the typical party scene. In fact, he had just founded Vanderbilt's only Christian fraternity, which I eagerly asked questions about and happily joined a few months later. That fraternity went on to change my life, teaching me the power of true brotherhood and holding me accountable to high Christian standards. It cultivated my faith and helped me overcome lifelong habitual sins. And it all began with the witness of one man helping me ask questions and long for more.

Years later while in law school, the same Baptist friend became a High Church Anglican. One day, he called me out of the blue and asked me what it was like being Catholic. I reminded him that I had been raised in the Church and had to fight for my faith in college since most of my friends were evangelicals or atheists. I told him about my love for liturgy and tradition. I didn't preach; I simply shared. He then told me about his latest foray into the early Church Fathers and asked all the right questions about the faith of the first Christians. I soon connected him with a solid priest who inspired him to become Catholic less than a year later. Soon after graduating from law school, he became a seminarian, and he is now only one step away from priestly ordination. In the end, our providential meeting during the first few days of my freshman year changed both our lives for the better. I entered into life-long Christian discipleship. He became a Catholic and will soon be a priest. It all began with curiosity and wonder.

It's amazing what happens when we slow down long enough to ask the right questions. All the great transformations in life begin with letting beauty speak so it can draw us into a posture of openness and receptivity.

I'll also never forget the chaos of buying my first home and inviting seven of my best friends to form an intentional community under the same roof. Or what it was like falling in love for the first time. Or starting a business without a clue of what I was doing. These moments were decision points, nothing less than calculated risks that pulled me out of indifference into action. Each began with a spirit of wonder and a simple question: *What was my life all about?*

The only danger in asking big questions is expecting quick answers. The truth seeker in all of us doesn't like to wait. There's a century-old letter by Rainer Maria Rilke (whose poetry profoundly shaped Pope Saint John Paul II's Theology of the Body[1]) that humbles me every time I read it. Though he writes the letter to a young poet, he eloquently challenges my own impatience and sense of entitlement:

> Have patience with everything that remains unsolved in your heart. Try to love the *questions themselves*, like locked

↳ the process

[1] Theology of the Body is a series of addresses given by Pope Saint John Paul II during his Wednesday audiences from September 1979 to November 1984. Additional information can be found on the website of the United States Conference of Catholic Bishops (USCCB) at https://www.usccb.org/issues -and-action/marriage-and-family/natural-family-planning/catholic-teaching /theology-of-the-body.

rooms and like books written in a foreign language. Do not now look for the answers. They cannot now be given to you because you could not live them. It is a question of experiencing everything. At present you need to *live* the question. Perhaps you will gradually, without even noticing it, find yourself experiencing the answer, some distant day.[2]

Some questions are full of infinite mystery and demand lifelong contemplation. Others are simple and progressive, building upon previous insights. But all the best questions in life must be *lived* with intentionality and wonder.

Until I attended college, I had lived obediently but not intentionally. I knew how to please parents, teachers, coaches, and friends. I played on a state championship football team with a star quarterback who went on to become the youngest head coach in NFL history. I dated the girl of my eighteen-year-old dreams and enjoyed decent academic success. But I wasn't living for anything bigger than myself. I wasn't asking philosophical questions or dreaming beyond my own ego. When I moved to Nashville and started college, I began looking for more. More importantly, I began *wondering* for the first time what it meant to be human and why I was alive at this particular moment in history.

None of us can ask (much less explore) the big questions of life without wonder. With wonder comes a spirit of humble contemplation, a thirst for knowledge and truth, a deep sense that life is charged with grandeur.

What is your life all about? Do you have a profound sense of freedom and purpose when you get out of bed in the morning? Are work and leisure integrated in your

[2] Rainer Maria Rilke, *Letters to a Young Poet: The Possibility of Being*, trans. Joan M. Burnham (New York: MJF Books, 2000), p. 35 (emphasis in original).

life? Do your friends bring out the best in you? Are you actively discerning or living your life mission?

We will dive into these questions in the principles that follow, but first we have to decide once and for all that we want to live intentionally. No more idle drifting. No more passive acceptance. No more living without *wonder.*

We are made to ask the big questions of life with childlike trust, to have a holy curiosity that enables us to think deeply and stand in awe. This spirit of wonder is the great pathway to knowledge and love. It's a window into the heart of God, who, as G. K. Chesterton observes, "has the eternal appetite of infancy; for we have sinned and grown old, and our Father is younger than we."[3] Only with this spirit of wonder can we allow beauty to lead us to truth and ultimately to God himself. Otherwise, we easily fall into a Stoic or Pharisaical approach to life. By teaching us to long for things seemingly beyond our reach, beauty protects us against pride and false self-sufficiency. It leads to humility born of wonder.

noticing how small we are + how much we have to learn

HUMILITY BORN OF WONDER

During the summer of 2020, we lived through a nonstop season of racial tension and violent riots across the world. From the streets of Minneapolis to London, demands for justice resounded in search for answers. Others took this demand for justice and twisted it into their own agendas, setting historic churches and government buildings aflame. City-wide curfews were instituted as retail stores were shamelessly looted. Social media was a mob scene, and mainstream news was as divided and contentious as ever.

[3] G. K. Chesterton, *Orthodoxy* (Nashville: Love Good, 2017), p. 73.

Amid all this social unrest, rare were the prophetic voices reminding us to humble ourselves before God and each other. Rare were the bold invitations to prayer and fasting. How many of us allowed curiosity and *wonder* to lead to loving dialogue rather than simply alleviating our consciences with virtue signaling? To live with wonder implies that we don't have all the answers. We don't have to be experts on every issue that comes across our news feed. We don't have to give into the constant noise of our modern society that anesthetizes our desire for beauty and truth. Big events and social media engagement should never be a priority over soul-to-soul evangelization. How many times have we fallen into the trap of thinking that activity is more powerful than prayer or that shouting is more effective than loving dialogue?

If noise goes hand-in-hand with pride, wonder goes hand-in-hand with humility. We must let beauty speak to our hearts as wonder breaks down the walls, heightens our sensitivities, and prepares us to encounter God in others. According to Robert Cardinal Sarah,

> Our world no longer hears God because it is constantly speaking, at a devastating speed and volume, in order to say nothing. Modern civilization does not know how to be quiet.... Noise is a deceptive, addictive, and false tranquilizer. The tragedy of our world is never better summed up than in the fury of senseless noise that stubbornly hates silence. This age detests the things that silence bring us to: encounter, wonder, and kneeling before God.[4]

Wonder, humility, and silence go hand-in-hand. They are the great antidotes for a world obsessed with noise.

[4] Robert Cardinal Sarah, *The Power of Silence against the Dictatorship of Noise*, trans. Michael J. Miller (San Francisco: Ignatius Press, 2017), p. 56.

They counteract political ideology and celebrity worship. They ignite genuine creativity among artists and profound wisdom among civic leaders. They also remind us that we cannot save ourselves and that we are simply God's unprofitable servants.

To have a world that is true, good, and beautiful, we must sit in silence long enough to hunger for more. We must cultivate humility born of wonder. Romano Guardini, whose rich theology deeply influenced the last three popes, argues:

> The greatest things are accomplished in silence—not in the clamor and display of superficial eventfulness, but in the deep clarity of inner vision; in the almost imperceptible start of decision, in quiet overcoming and hidden sacrifice. Spiritual conception happens when the heart is quickened by love, and the free will stirs to action. The silent forces are the strong forces.[5]

Talk about counterintuitive and countercultural. While few of us are called to be brilliant theologians or eloquent preachers, all of us are called to engage the silent forces within us that inspire the world to long for more. It's not about having all the right answers but rather stirring up all the right questions. When our family and friends see us living with humility born of wonder, we trigger the infinite desire built into their souls. As we radiate the beauty of God's love in the world, they become curious and want what we have. They wonder what's different about us and start asking all the right questions about what it means to be human. And this is where true evangelization begins.

[5] Romano Guardini, *The Lord*, trans. Elinor Castendyk Briefs (Washington, DC: Regnery Publishing, 2014), p. 15.

If you're tempted to think that being an apostle means making splendid arguments on well-known blogs, never tire of returning to wonder. If you're tempted to think that being an apostle is synonymous with social justice or political action, never tire of returning to wonder. Your life can include all those things, but you'll remain forever ineffective without humility born of wonder.

Humility is not only a sign of wonder; it's the precursor to joy. It's the posture necessary to perceive beauty and enjoy it wholeheartedly. It's the posture necessary for any pursuit of truth. No child jumps out of a tree into his father's arms without humility and trust. No Christian enters into the joy of salvation without humility and wonder.

How can you cultivate a posture of receptivity to this great gift of wonder? It doesn't require hobbit holes or summer camps. It isn't limited to life-changing books or brilliant symphonies. And it certainly isn't facilitated by political parties or social media platforms. Cultivating wonder can be as heroic as giving up technology for a month or as simple as reading great literature every night before going to bed.

C. S. Lewis wrote famously in *The Weight of Glory* that "we do not want merely to see beauty, though, God knows, even that is bounty enough. We want something else which can hardly be put into words—to be united with the beauty we see, to pass into it, to receive it into ourselves, to bathe in it, to become part of it."[6] Once wonder has led to beauty and reminded us that we're made for more, we can't help but want to become one with the beauty we've encountered. And there's only one way to do that: become one with its Source.

[6] C. S. Lewis, *The Weight of Glory and Other Addresses* (New York: Harper-One, 2001), p. 42.

THE ARROW OF BEAUTY

In one of his first major writings to the Christian faithful, Pope Francis shares that "every expression of true beauty can thus be acknowledged as a path leading to an encounter with the Lord Jesus."[7] Indeed, every encounter with beauty is an encounter with God and a foretaste of heaven. Across every denomination and generation of Christians, beauty has great power to deepen our conversion and inspire our work of evangelization. By cultivating a habitual spirit of wonder, we open ourselves up to this beauty that so powerfully unites us with each other and most importantly with God himself.

Pope Benedict XVI similarly mused, "To me art and the Saints are the greatest apologetic for our faith."[8] He's one of the most important theologians of the past century, and yet he doesn't look to Aquinas' five proofs for the existence of God or the Church's preferential option for the poor to be convinced of the Gospel. He looks to beauty. He cultivates wonder. And it's more than just standing in awe of the Sistine Chapel or Beethoven's *Requiem Mass*. As I shared in this book's introduction, it's the beauty of the saints and their intimate union with God that most convinces our former pope of the claims of Christianity.

In one of his great speeches on beauty, Benedict XVI uses the analogy of an arrow to explain how it wounds our

---

[7] Francis, Apostolic Exhortation on the Proclamation of the Gospel in Today's World *Evangelii Gaudium* (November 24, 2013), no. 167, http://www.vatican.va/content/francesco/en/apost_exhortations/documents/papa-francesco_esortazione-ap_20131124_evangelii-gaudium.html.

[8] Benedict XVI, Meeting with the Clergy of the Diocese of Bolzano-Bressanone (August 6, 2008), http://www.vatican.va/content/benedict-xvi/en/speeches/2008/august/documents/hf_ben-xvi_spe_20080806_clero-bressanone.html.

souls and points us back to God, who is the Author of all that is true, good, and beautiful. At one point, he shares a quote from fourteenth-century Byzantine theologian Nicholas Cabasilas:

> When men have a longing so great that it surpasses human nature and eagerly desire and are able to accomplish things beyond human thought, it is the Bridegroom who has smitten them with this longing. It is he who has sent a ray of his beauty into their eyes. The greatness of the wound already shows the arrow which has struck home, the longing indicates who has inflicted the wound.[9]

If beauty is the arrow, wonder is the sharpening stone. Wonder jealously guards our childlike response to beauty. It keeps our hearts pure and vulnerable so that beauty can wound us with maximum impact. Think about the Blessed Mother at the moment of the Annunciation. What role did wonder play in her openness and receptivity to the archangel Gabriel and eventual overshadowing of the Holy Spirit that led to the Incarnation?

Without wonder, our hearts grow cold to the endless encounters with beauty placed before us every day. We become closed off to the promptings of the Holy Spirit so necessary for our sanctification and the salvation of others. As great Dominicans have always reminded me, wonder leads to knowledge and knowledge leads to love. Without wonder, the Christian life cannot get off the ground, much less progress to its full potential.

---

[9] Congregation for the Doctrine of the Faith, *Message of His Eminence Card. Joseph Ratzinger to the Communion and Liberation (CL) Meeting at Rimini (24–30 August 2002)*, quoting Nicholas Cabasilas, *The Life in Christ*, Second Book, 15, http://www.vatican.va/roman_curia/congregations/cfaith/documents/rc_con_cfaith_doc_20020824_ratzinger-cl-rimini_en.html.

For years I've had the privilege of leading annual pilgrimages to Rome with young people from the United States and England. Most recently, I was struck by how quickly a group of young men from Indiana latched onto the idea of becoming great saints together, of striving for their full potential in the Christian life. Every day I took them to the tombs of great mystics and martyrs like Saint Catherine of Siena, Saint Philip Neri, Saint Cecilia, and even Saints Peter and Paul. Every night, their hearts were full of wonder as they dreamed about transforming the world through the beauty of holiness.

Has there ever been a more obvious need for great saints to rise up in the splendor of holiness and point the world back to God? Is there anything more worthy of our pursuit than the eternal prize of heaven, where we'll spend eternity contemplating the very beauty of God himself? In today's culture of noise, we always run the risk of letting beauty remain a whimsical concept at arm's length. It must be incarnated into our lives through childlike wonder so it can pierce our hearts and elevate our souls. Then, and only then, does beauty wound us so that we can't help but trace the arrow back to its Source. That longing, that wound, that infinite desire ultimately points to God himself. Whether encountered through music, art, or the witness of an aspiring saint, beauty is always a glimpse into the Father's heart.

RETURN TO HOBBITON

On a return trip to New Zealand more than two years ago, I was in the city of Wellington with a few young people who wanted to treat me to a night of live music at the local botanical gardens. Before long we were exploring the full breadth of the gardens on a search for glow worms. Being from the American South, I assumed I was looking for something akin to lightning bugs. But I was in store for a wondrous surprise.

They told me to keep quiet and turn off my phone. As we penetrated the darkness with nothing but wonder in our hearts, I began to think they were all playing a prank on me. *Where and when was this adventure going to end? Were they about to lead me off the path into a hidden body of water? Was someone about to jump from behind a bush and scare the living daylights out of me?*

The farther we moved down the path, the more skeptical I became. I was nervous and uncomfortable. Suddenly, I heard someone whisper, "Over here!" and I followed the sound of her voice. She told me to look closely at the embankment. With my nose nearly touching the dirt, my eyes slowly adjusted until I could see a massive constellation of glow worms. It felt less like I was looking down at the dirt and more like I was looking up at the stars. Everything in me came alive. In this moment, my senses were awakened as I encountered the beauty of God's creation. Though it was my fourth trip to New Zealand in three years, I was left in a state of wonder yet again. As it turns out, beauty is ever ancient and ever new.

The only danger in letting wonder run wild is the possibility of slipping into fantasy rather than staying rooted in reality. I'm not referring to fantasy as a literary genre but as *nonreality*, when wonder leads to unfettered dreams that degrade into idols. Therefore, we need virtue to temper our wonder, which is the foundation for the principle of *freedom*, which will be discussed in the next chapter.

Suffice it to say that, without wonder, we'll never encounter the beauty we long for that prompts us to ask life's most important questions. We'll forget that we're made for more. Our first task in the art of being human is to reclaim our imagination and slow down long enough to stand in awe before the mysteries of life.

What am I made for? Where did I come from? Where am I going? These are the humble questions of philosophers and poets, but they become our questions as well with a little dose of childlike wonder.

Last time I was struck was by looking back at all the times God reached out to me

GETTING PRACTICAL

- Go for a hike or spend time in nature this week. Let the beauty of God's creation enlarge your soul and heighten your sense of wonder.
- Be intentional about curating music, books, movies, and art that keep your wonder alive. Life is too short to be a passive consumer.
- Keep *The Chronicles of Narnia* by C. S. Lewis, *The Lord of the Rings* by J. R. R. Tolkien, and other Gospel-infused fantasy on rotation for bedside reading. When possible, read them aloud to children.
- Make your next trip more of a pilgrimage than a vacation. Where you go doesn't matter as much as how well you cultivate beauty, adventure, and a sense of wonder.
- Go on an extended technology fast, giving up social media and screen entertainment except when necessary for school or work. A three-week fast may change your habits, but a three-month fast will change your life.

FURTHER READING

Dubay, Thomas, S.M. *The Evidential Power of Beauty: Science and Theology Meet.* San Francisco: Ignatius Press, 1999.

Kreeft, Peter. *Philosophy 101 by Socrates: An Introduction to Philosophy via Plato's Apology.* San Francisco: Ignatius Press, 2012.

Peterson, Andrew. *The Wingfeather Saga.* Books 1–4. Colorado Springs: WaterBrook, 2021.

Pieper, Josef. *Only the Lover Sings: Art and Contemplation.* Translated by Lothar Krauth. San Francisco: Ignatius Press, 1990.

Chapter 2

Freedom

'frēdəm | noun | the state of not being imprisoned or enslaved.

My jaw dropped as I read the sign outside of a castle in Edinburgh, Scotland, describing the brutal death of William Wallace at the hands of the British more than seven hundred years ago. I was a college student studying abroad, and there was no telling how many times I had seen *Braveheart* at that point. As far as I was concerned, the film defined masculine genius, making William Wallace everything I wanted to be in life. However, hearing that he had been hanged, drawn, and quartered with body parts scattered across England was a little more history than I was ready for that day.

I spent most of my time abroad studying philosophy at University College London. Narrowly avoiding René Descartes and other modern philosophers, I focused my studies on the writings of canonized saints. Between reading excerpts of Saint Augustine's *Confessions* for the first time and studying the *Summa Theologiae* by Saint Thomas Aquinas, my intellectual development was in good hands. On top of that, I had class only two days a week, which afforded me five-day weekends to explore Europe on discount airlines. These were unforgettable months, full of cheap wine and fancy cigars in cities all over the continent of my heritage. I learned that parts of my personality were enshrined in the English, Irish, Scottish, and German cultures from which I came. I learned what it meant to be protected by God's grace while skiing the Swiss Alps and while searching for late-night hostels in Paris. I explored catacombs in Rome, waited hours to see the pope in Munich, and craned my neck as I took in the full majesty of La Sagrada Familia in Barcelona. The entire semester was an adventure in self-forgetfulness and self-discovery.

What, then, was so powerful about my brief encounter with the legacy of William Wallace that day in Scotland? Of all the spectacular moments of that time abroad, my one day in Edinburgh was filled with gray skies, crammed pubs, and rambunctious personalities with difficult-to-understand accents. Yet, something about William Wallace left my heart burning. What did the Scottish and arguably their most famous knight teach me about freedom that day?

THEY CAN TAKE OUR LIVES

The year was 1297, and William Wallace had just begun his rebellion against the English in pursuit of Scottish independence. He was a patriot, a proud Scotsman seeking to liberate his homeland. He fought and won many battles against the English before being captured and ultimately killed for high treason by King Edward I. Long before the 1995 release of Mel Gibson's film, his valiant fight for freedom was memorialized in a several-hundred-page poem called *The Wallace*. In fact, apart from the Bible, it was the most popular book in Scotland for several hundred years after its publication.[1]

---

[1] *Encyclopædia Britannica*, s.v. "William Wallace", last updated August 2022, https://www.britannica.com/biography/William-Wallace.

What is it about freedom fighters that inspires something deep in every human heart? Why do we unsheathe our swords and unleash our prayers in support of the great liberators of every human era? Why do their stories continue to stir our imagination and advance the cause of freedom long after their heroic lives and often untimely deaths?

William Wallace, like rebels against the establishment of every age, knew that true freedom demanded sacrifice. It demanded courage, what Chesterton called a "strong desire to live taking the form of a readiness to die".[2] Wallace exercised the kind of interior freedom that rejected all forms of apathy, enslavement, and fear. He fought without paying attention to the wounds. He toiled without rest. In the end, his bravery cost him his life.

We often reduce freedom to mere license, being able to do whatever we want, whenever we want, with whomever we want. This flattened view of liberty is what many people espouse in democratic societies, attempting to advance freedom without making any sacrifices. Freedom that has been reduced to license quickly devolves into licentiousness. Look at ancient Rome. Look at modern America. Every licentious society trades freedom for self-absorption. Enslaved by their base desires, the citizens of such a society can turn in on themselves, seeking comfort until they become incapable of heroic sacrifice.

Am I any different? Every day, I battle against my own base desires. I'm still attached to passions that have only led to self-destruction in the past. If I don't have the ability to say no to these passions, will I ever know true freedom? Will I ever be capable of heroic sacrifice and selfless love?

Having spent much of his life under Communist rule in Poland, Pope Saint John Paul II appreciated the priceless gift of freedom. When he came to America in 1995 and

[2] G.K. Chesterton, *Orthodoxy* (Nashville: Love Good, 2017), p. 115.

celebrated Mass at Oriole Park in Baltimore, he gave an impassioned plea to all Americans to build freedom upon the foundation of truth:

> America has always wanted to be a land of the free. Today, the challenge facing America is to find freedom's fulfillment in the truth: the truth that is intrinsic to human life created in God's image and likeness, the truth that is written on the human heart, the truth that can be known by reason and can therefore form the basis of a profound and universal dialogue among people about the direction they must give to their lives and their activities.... We must guard the truth that is the condition of authentic freedom, the truth that allows freedom to be fulfilled in goodness. We must guard the *deposit of divine truth handed down to us in the Church*, especially in view of the challenges posed by a materialistic culture and by a permissive mentality that reduces freedom to license.[3]

Rare are the political, religious, and cultural leaders who reject comfort or sacrifice their reputations for sake of the truth. Rare are the activists who live for a cause truly greater than themselves. Our society values comfort, power, and pleasure above all else. And yet, continued John Paul II, true "freedom consists not in doing what we like, but in having the right to do what we ought."[4] Freedom without truth is slavery to our base desires. Endless options are worthless if they're fundamentally deficient.

When did you first learn the importance of self-denial in your own life? Did you grow up with family or friends

---

[3] John Paul II, Apostolic Journey to the United States of America: Eucharistic Celebration in Oriole Park at Camden Yards, Baltimore (homily, October 8, 1995), nos. 6, 8 (emphasis in original), https://www.vatican.va/content/john-paul-ii/en/homilies/1995/documents/hf_jp-ii_hom_19951008_baltimore.html.

[4] Ibid., no. 7.

who lived with deep interior freedom? How often did you fall into the age-old trap of equating liberty with license, particularly when you were younger?

There was something about playing football from a young age that taught me the importance of self-denial, whether I liked it or not. It's a small miracle that I didn't quit before the lesson was engrained in my soul.

JOYFUL SELF-MASTERY

"Don't give up yet," my dad repeated in earnest as we drove home from the local neighborhood park. There was something calm and reassuring in his voice. "You've only just begun. Workouts will get easier as you get into better shape, and you'll soon have no regrets. Just give yourself a little more time."

It was a ruthlessly hot and humid day in north Georgia, and I was in the middle of my first week of football practice in the fourth grade. My eyes were still red and my nose still runny. I was an exhausted mess. Nothing in me wanted to go back the next day and face my fears again. I felt completely uninspired and inadequate. Why would anyone want to strap on pads and pound on each other day after day? If I couldn't avoid the sport, surely I could at least wait a few more years before playing competitively.

Fourth and fifth grade passed. I was toughening up. Slowly football was becoming a huge part of life. I was growing in my freedom as an athlete, able to compete at a much higher level as I came to know the game better and grew in strength and skill. By the time I was in middle school, I had a head start on most of my teammates. I wasn't afraid to throw myself into linebackers and collide with running backs in an open field. For several years, I started on both sides of the ball and began seeing my personality and confidence develop on and off the field. It was the gentle reassurances from Dad and the unconditional love from Mom that kept me moving forward when I wanted to quit. And it was the many lessons learned along the way that transformed football into something deeply meaningful and transformative.

Eight grueling and gratifying seasons later, I stood alongside fifty of my closest friends as state champions. It was my senior year of high school, and football had become a treasured part of my life. It had taught me the value of brotherhood and virtue, the thrill of victory and the agony of defeat, the need for diversity of gifts and unity of purpose. As we stood on the fifty yard line singing our alma mater at the end of that championship game, snow began to fall unexpectedly (something that never happened in Atlanta that time of year). Suddenly, memories from my first week of practice in fourth grade came rushing back, and I was smiling with pure gratitude and joy. Every grueling exercise, painful injury, and heartbreaking loss over the course of those nine seasons felt worth it.

Freedom without restraint isn't freedom at all. True freedom is built on joyful self-mastery. It's built on self-denial and sacrifice. Long before a warrior or a martyr or a football player has the courage to sacrifice for his cause, he's already died a thousand deaths in pursuit of virtue. In fact, he doesn't have the freedom to reach his full potential until he's spent years in preparation and practice. This kind of interior freedom rooted in virtue is the only way to elevate us beyond fleeting pleasures that hold us back from our full potential. It's also our only rock-solid foundation for the intellectual, moral, and political freedom necessary for human flourishing.

Do you want to live with true interior freedom? Do you long for the peace that comes with a rightly ordered soul? Do you want to reach your full potential spiritually, physically, and morally?

You can't do it without virtue.

WHY VIRTUE MATTERS

Virtues are good habits that help us choose the highest good at any given moment with ease and joy. Sadly, we live in a world today that has replaced virtue with values. "You have your values, and I have mine," say most people as they come into conflict with others. This to-each-his-own mentality allows political correctness to overshadow moral integrity. It allows toxic sentimentality to invade the culture and even the Church. It eliminates objective standards. Truth, and by extension *freedom*, is compromised.

Meanwhile, this moral relativism allows our infinite hunger for God to wither away. It strangles our freedom by convincing us that any universal statement about *how to live* is an imposition. In light of so much confusion, there is a profound need to understand virtue and its rootedness in objective truth.

According to philosopher Alasdair MacIntyre, "There is no way to possess the virtues except as part of a tradition in which we inherit them."[5] Of course, there's a long-standing Christian tradition of approaching morality through this lens. With the help of Aristotle and Aquinas, MacIntyre boldly proposes that virtue is the only way to talk about goodness and happiness:

> For what constitutes the good for man is a complete human life lived at its best, and the exercise of the virtues

[5] Alasdair MacIntyre, *After Virtue* (Notre Dame, IN: University of Notre Dame Press, 2007), p. 149.

is a necessary and central part of such a life, not a mere preparatory exercise to secure such a life. We thus cannot characterize the good for man adequately without already having made reference to the virtues. And within an Aristotelian framework, the suggestion therefore that there might be some means to achieve the good for man without the exercise of the virtues makes no sense.[6]

Indeed, happiness is inseparable from virtue. There is no lasting joy without interior freedom. This was God's design from the beginning. At what point, then, did everything go awry? The story, of course, can be traced back to the fall of man in the Garden of Eden (Gen 3) when Adam and Eve did the *one thing* God asked them not to do by eating from the tree of knowledge of good and evil. Satan convinced them that they could become like God without God. Their sin was our sin. They disobeyed our Creator and rejected his love, severely wounding their relationship with him, each other, and the rest of creation. The human intellect became darkened, the will weakened, and the passions disordered. From that point on, Original Sin inhibited our ability to see the good clearly and embrace it with love. Until the end of time, the good would now have to be fought for with virtue aided by grace.

Without virtue, we will never find freedom from the effects of Original Sin or be truly happy. In this sense, virtue and freedom are synonymous. Virtue brings freedom and peace to our soul, what Saint Augustine describes as a "tranquility of order", in which everything is in its proper place.[7] In the words of our Lord, we must "seek first his kingdom and his righteousness, and all these things shall

[6] Ibid.
[7] Augustine, *City of God* XIX, 13, trans. Ford Lewis Battles (Pittsburgh: Pittsburgh Theological Seminary, 1973).

be yours as well" (Mt 6:33). Virtue, aided by grace, makes it easy for us to seek God's kingdom as the highest Good. With that proper ordering in our souls comes a profound peace beyond all understanding.

There are many different virtues that help us achieve this freedom. Before we dive into the cardinal virtues of temperance, justice, fortitude, and prudence, it's important to recognize humility as their foundation. As an overflow of our previous principle of *wonder*, humility is a healthy self-forgetfulness that seeks the good of others above our own. It acknowledges our gifts and limitations. With the help of humility, we're open to change and personal growth. This is exactly where the rubber meets the road if we are serious about dying to ourselves and allowing Christ to live within us. Once we're committed to humility, growth in all the virtues becomes possible.

THE CARDINAL VIRTUES

The idea of virtue or moral excellence is as old as Western civilization. One of the first-ever expositions on virtue comes from Plato's *Republic*, in which he organizes all virtues under four categories called the cardinal virtues.[8] According to Alasdair MacIntyre, Plato's concept of virtue presupposes a "unity of the virtues" that places "each virtue in a total harmonious scheme of human life".[9] The cardinal virtues of temperance, justice, fortitude, and prudence are totally interdependent on each other. They're also the four categories under which all other human virtues fall.

---

[8] Plato, *Republic* IV, 2, from *Plato's Republic: A Critical Guide*, ed. Mark L. McPherran (Cambridge: Cambridge University Press, 2013).

[9] MacIntyre, *After Virtue*, p. 149.

First, according to the *Catechism of the Catholic Church*, temperance is the "moral virtue that moderates the attraction of pleasures and provides balance in the use of created goods".[10] It's best summed up as self-control. We often use the word to mean abstinence from alcohol, but it encompasses other virtues like chastity and patience. It helps us flee evil and love good in the face of temptation. It's a common struggle for those of us who are young, for "the spirit indeed is willing, but the flesh is weak" (Mt 26:41). In a culture that's gone soft, it's easy to justify comfort and even debauchery. However, self-restraint has always been a key ingredient to my own personal happiness. Every time I slip into impurity, gluttony, or immoderation of any kind, I always end up miserable. On the other hand, temperance has only brought me joy.

Secondly, the cardinal virtue of justice means giving others their due, providing the foundation for moral and civil laws, among other things. Aquinas defines justice as "nothing else than to render to each one his own".[11] It also entails virtues like religion (whereby we worship God who created and redeemed us) and patriotism (whereby we love our homeland even to the point of death). Justice is a widely celebrated virtue. At least in theory, it's the basis for every law that's ever passed and every protest that's ever taken place. It's the building block of family life and friendship. Ultimately, it's the cardinal virtue that provides the foundation for every Judeo-Christian society.

Thirdly, fortitude is the cardinal virtue that swells your heart with courage in the face of adversity, what C. S. Lewis describes as "not simply one of the virtues but the form

---

[10] *Catechism of the Catholic Church*, no. 1809.
[11] Aquinas, *Summa Theologiae* II-II, q. 58, art. 11.

of every virtue at the testing point".[12] Without fortitude carrying you through temptation or trial, you can never know how truly just or temperate you are. Without fortitude, you cannot overcome difficulties or setbacks. Think of every great athlete who ever lived. Think of every hero who ever sacrificed himself for love of his cause. They had to overcome fear, exhaustion, insecurity, and selfishness. From the most heroic acts to the most basic, every virtuous deed depends on fortitude.

Finally, prudence is right reason in action. It's the charioteer of the virtues that keeps everything else in line. All the greatest leaders are masters of prudence. They know what to do, how and when to do it, and who to involve. It's more than mere knowledge or skill. It's wisdom built on experience. Of all the cardinal virtues, prudence is the one I struggle with the most because my zeal often gets the better of me. I forget to slow down and think things through. Similarly, there's likely a cardinal virtue that you struggle with most based on your temperament. However, your struggles can also change based on circumstances and seasons of life.

These hinge virtues lay the natural foundation for the theological virtues of faith, hope, and love, which are gifts infused by God. As grace builds on nature, temperance and fortitude lead to heroic self-sacrifice, justice becomes mercy, and prudence is transformed into divine wisdom. Nothing more powerfully maximizes our faith, hope, and love than a solid foundation in natural virtue. We'll dive deeper into faith under the principle of *prayer* and hope under the principle of *suffering*. Love will also come up continually in the chapters ahead, with a particular emphasis under the principle of *mission*.

---

[12] C. S. Lewis, *The Screwtape Letters: With Screwtape Proposes a Toast* (New York: HarperOne, 2013), p. 161.

It's crucial to remember that virtue is not self-reliance but self-mastery, as it trains our hearts to aim for the highest good that is ultimately God himself. As our repulsion for evil grows, so does our distaste for lesser goods. As we cultivate this interior freedom built on virtue, mere license to do whatever we want appears increasingly ridiculous. Yet, there are countless forces in our post-Christian culture working against our interior freedom. It's not easy to strive for the highest ideals in today's world, and there are few arenas of human culture where this struggle is more clearly seen than technology.

ATTACKS ON FREEDOM

In her most recent book, Harvard professor Shoshana Zuboff coins the phrase *surveillance capitalism* in reference to big tech companies like Facebook, Amazon, and Google.[13] While these platforms may be free to use, she proposes that they endanger true human freedom. They're built to turn consumers into addicts and customers into commodities. According to Zuboff, they buy, sell, and manipulate our behavior in a way that "produces a psychic numbing that inures us to the realities of being tracked, parsed, mined, and modified".[14] Dangerously, we may even realize the force of manipulation behind these platforms and do nothing about it because of our psychological dependency on them. Zuboff hauntingly predicts:

> Just as industrial civilization flourished at the expense of nature and now threatens to cost us the Earth, an information civilization shaped by surveillance capitalism

---

[13] Shoshana Zuboff, *The Age of Surveillance Capitalism: The Fight for a Human Future at the New Frontier of Power* (New York: PublicAffairs, 2020).

[14] Ibid., p. 11.

and its new instrumentarian power will thrive at the expense of human nature and will threaten to cost us our humanity.[15]

I was a freshman at Vanderbilt when Facebook first became available, and the world was a very different place. At the time, we were one of twenty universities that had access to the platform. We were guinea pigs for Mark Zuckerberg and companions to work out the kinks. It was still a very simple form of social media, with users posting brief messages on their home pages and occasionally sending direct messages to each other. It was a glorified version of Myspace and a sophisticated upgrade to AOL Instant Messenger. The iPhone hadn't been released yet, so we could access Facebook only from a computer. I'll never forget my disappointment when it became available to other university students and eventually to high school students as well. It was then easy to see the trajectory. Facebook was intended for the entire world. Today, there are close to two billion daily active users.[16] Facebook is more powerful and influential than many national governments, which is to say nothing of Snapchat, TikTok, and other new platforms growing in popularity by the day.

Yet, most people don't think twice about the number of hours they spend on social media. They assume that their time spent behind screens or even their sins committed in isolation are harmless. In a world that has normalized apathy and indecency, we need freedom fighters as never before. We need brave men and women who will rise up in the splendor of truth and fight for the proliferation of virtue yet again.

[15] Ibid., pp. 11–12.

[16] Statista, "Number of Daily Active Facebook Users Worldwide as of 2nd Quarter 2022", July 28, 2022, https://www. statista.com/statistics/346167 /facebook-global-dau/.

Post-Christian culture, like any culture without Christ as its integrating principle, has a way of attacking personal freedom on every front. What's our response? Who are the William Wallaces of this age who will reject the growing soft totalitarianism? Who is virtuous enough to reject their base desires that thwart their full potential? Are there enough of us longing to live with freedom, joy, and integrity?

HEROIC VIRTUE

Imagine your soul rightly ordered, with virtue springing forth in the face of every temptation. Imagine having an interior freedom that effortlessly chooses the good and inspires others to do the same. Imagine finding it easy to be humble, generous, and selfless. This is the good life. This is the return to Eden. This is the proper response to a God who holds out infinite joy.

Few things captivate the world faster than interior freedom. No one ever sees it coming. If you want your lifestyle to inspire others, you must be a man or woman of virtue. In a world full of egoism, confusion, and despair, virtue is beautiful beyond description. It breeds honest self-assessment by reminding us that we have sins that need to be forgiven through reconciliation. It reminds us that we have disordered desires and inclinations that need to be healed and purified in prayer. Virtue also increases our awareness of weaknesses and gifts. It helps us more effectively discern God's will (which is the basis for our ninth principle of *mission*) and live in *community* with others (our seventh principle).

As I mentioned previously, for me college was a time of testing the waters and asking big life questions. Once beauty awakened my heart, I began to live differently. I didn't want to miss a moment. Wonder became less of a conscious principle and more of a constant instinct, making life exhilarating and vivid. I was done with living passively and wanted everything to be charged with purpose and intention. However, with the endless adventures came endless vocational questions that I found impossible to navigate without virtue: *Should I go to work in the music industry? Should I marry the next solid Catholic woman I date? Should I become a priest?* I thought I was chasing after higher and higher goods only to become increasingly aware of my inability to hold them with open hands. I had attachments everywhere but wasn't ready to commit anywhere. The gift of wonder had turned life into an adventure, but without a proper understanding of human freedom, it had often mutated into paralysis or self-absorption.

What I needed then is the same thing I need now: deeply rooted virtue that holds the middle ground and protects my freedom to pursue what is true, good, and beautiful. Always lying in the middle, virtue isn't found in extremes like puritanism or gluttony, cowardice or recklessness. It's not a concession of desire but a constancy of disposition that increases interior freedom. It's an ever-deepening embrace of the highest good, a reintegration of the soul.

Long before the Church considers canonizing a saint, she begins by confirming that the individual has lived with heroic virtue.[17] Not any old virtue but *heroic* virtue. It's the precondition for opening the cause for any saint's canonization. In a world as morally far-gone as ours, we need a vast array of heroes who are ready to free us from the bonds of complacency. In the words of Bishop Robert Barron, "Each of the saints, in his or her own

[17] *Catechism of the Catholic Church*, no. 828.

utterly unique manner, shows forth some aspect of God's beauty and perfection. God makes saints the way he makes plants and animals and stars: exuberantly, effervescently, and with a preference for wild diversity."[18] There's no limit to what this heroic virtue can look like because God created each of us for our specific time, place, and situation. We must be those modern-day saints who are creative and generous in how we lay down our egos and rise up in defense of all that makes life worth living.

If we want to cultivate the art of being human, we must be powerhouses of interior freedom and heroic virtue. In fact, our next principle of *friendship* presupposes an understanding of virtue because its highest form requires a common pursuit of excellence. Like all of the principles that follow, true friendship depends on interior freedom. It's also the foundation for living the faith and sharing it with others, ensuring that we first captivate others with integrity so that we have credibility when we preach the Gospel. What could possibly be more beautiful in a world caught up in the misery of sin? What stands in more stark contrast to our comfortable, pleasure-seeking society? Interior freedom is the way out of our cultural malaise. Over time, it will not only restore our moral backbone as a society. It will plant seeds of lasting fruit that will bring a glimpse of Eden back to Earth.

GETTING PRACTICAL

- Examine your conscience every night before you go to bed. Become aware of the gap between who you are and who you want to be.

[18] Robert Barron, *Letter to a Suffering Church: A Bishop Speaks on the Sexual Abuse Crisis* (Park Ridge, IL: Word on Fire, 2019), p. 77.

- Initiate a conversation about virtue with a family member or friend. Ask for his perspective and listen before you offer your own.
- Do something new that could lead to failure. The more courage you have to fail, the more courage you'll have to take risks and eventually do the impossible.
- Find a mentor or close friend who can help you identify your predominant strengths and faults. Ask for ongoing accountability and support.
- Fast once a week (e.g., eating one meal that day instead of three) and give up snacks, desserts, and alcohol for extended periods of thirty days or more. If you say no to good things now, you will have more strength to say no to evil things later.

FURTHER READING

Kreeft, Peter. *Back to Virtue: Traditional Moral Wisdom for Modern Moral Confusion*. San Francisco: Ignatius Press, 1992.

MacIntyre, Alasdair. *After Virtue*. Notre Dame IN: University of Notre Dame Press, 2007.

Pieper, Josef. *The Christian Idea of Man*. Translated by Dan Farrelly. South Bend, IN: St. Augustine's Press, 2011.

Sheen, Fulton J. *On Being Human: Reflections on Life and Living*. Garden City, NY: Doubleday, 1982.

Sri, Edward. *The Art of Living: The Cardinal Virtues and the Freedom to Love*. San Francisco: Ignatius Press; Greenwood Village, CO: Augustine Institute, 2021.

Chapter 3

Friendship

'frendSHip | *noun* | *a state of mutual trust and support between friends.*

"Run, brothers! Run! Give it all you've got!" I shouted to three of my closest friends as we hastily approached the busiest train station in Rome, Italy. We were in the middle of a two-week pilgrimage in Europe, and we were seconds away from missing the last train to our accommodations outside of town. The day was far spent, and we had lost track of time exploring basilicas, catacombs, and gelaterias. We now had two options before us: run like mad or spend the night on a park bench in the Eternal City.

We turned up the heat and sprinted with all our might, two of us making it onto the train's platform moments before the doors began closing. As we turned around, we saw one of our other friends fifty yards behind us. He was hustling, and it looked like he was going to make it in time. But our last friend was nowhere in sight. I panicked. *Should we board the train and hope for the best? Should we wait until all of us are together even if it means missing the train? Should we alert the conductor with the hopes of delaying our departure, even though European trains seem to never run late?*

As our second-to-last friend joined us on the platform, we were standing in a puddle of sweat and anxiety. If we missed the train home that night, we'd have a sleepless night and another day in the same dirty clothes. We'd also miss our only chance to grab the rosaries and prayer cards that we wanted the pope to bless the next day. But the only thing worse than not catching the train was losing our friend, so we waited as the anxiety mounted.

Ironically, this wasn't the first time we were exhausted and out of breath on this trip. Only a few days prior, we were climbing mountain peaks in Pollone, Italy, retracing the steps of one of our great heroes, Blessed Pier Giorgio Frassati. The hike came recommended by one of Frassati's living nieces. We were out of breath within the first fifteen minutes of it and lost within the first hour. Every time we thought we had arrived at a peak, it leveled off only to reveal another peak in the distance. It was hours before we finally gave up and traversed back down the side of the mountain. At one point, we stumbled into a beautiful church, but to this day I have no idea if it was the church that we had set out to find that morning.

Frassati was an avid hiker, friend of the poor, and devout Catholic who died in 1925. Pope John Paul II beatified him in 1990, bringing him one miracle away from canonization. Because we had the crazy privilege of spending an entire afternoon with his living relatives in Pollone, we heard all the stories of his early morning hikes to Mass. He used to wake up before his parents, slip out his bedroom window, and hike miles to a beautiful mountain parish. Over time, his most famous mantra, even among his friends, was *verso l'alto*, or "to the heights". He used it not only in the context of hiking but especially in the context of faith. For him, going to the heights of holiness was the noblest pursuit of all, and there was no one he wanted to do it with more than his friends.

Since we were having the adventure of a lifetime, my friends and I quickly embraced his mantra as our own and didn't hesitate to attempt the hike that morning. Whether the hike ended in success is debatable, but there's no doubt whatsoever that the inspiration to become great saints planted itself deep in our hearts that day. From that point forward, we knew beyond the shadow of a doubt that our common pursuit of heaven was the great link that bonded us together as friends.

Let's return again to the train station in Rome. What ever happened to our last friend who was racing to meet us on the platform so we could catch the last ride home? In a stroke of sheer providence, the train was delayed just long enough for him to arrive within seconds of its departure. In our group journal that chronicled the trip's adventures, we facetiously wrote, "One of us nearly died today." It was one of the more hilarious and notable memories of the pilgrimage, the entirety of which could be summed up by the phrase *verso l'alto*. To this day, these men remain the closest of friends—two of them now priests and the other well on his way as a seminarian studying in Rome.

What, then, are the key marks of genuine friendship, and what does it have to do with cultivating our humanity and spreading the Gospel? Is there a philosophy of friendship that we can embrace to help us find friends who are more than just circumstantial but intentional and even providential?

TO THE HEIGHTS

When you do a quick internet search of the word *friend*, you mostly find references to the most popular television show of the '90s starring Jennifer Aniston, Matthew Perry, and others. To put it bluntly, a storyline that glorifies casual sex with friends is anything but rooted in truth, beauty, and goodness. It's certainly not a model of genuine friendship that points us to the heights of our humanity.

Perhaps another place to start is the opening chapter of John Steinbeck's classic novella *Of Mice and Men*. The story follows the shared experiences of George Milton and Lennie Small, two displaced ranch workers in California struggling to find work during the Great Depression. They could not be more different from each other. George is "small and quick, dark of face, with restless eyes and sharp, strong features", while Lennie is a "huge man, shapeless of face", with the intellect of a child.[1] Though far from perfect, they are genuine friends. Within the first few pages of the book, a ritual between the two men clearly unfolds as George overcomes his impatience and takes on a rhythmic and reassuring tone with Lennie:

> "Guys like us, that work on ranches, are the loneliest guys in the world. They got no family. They don't belong no place. They come to ranch an' work up a stake and then they go inta town and blow their stake, and the first thing you know they're poundin' their tail on some other ranch. They ain't got nothing to look ahead to."
>
> Lennie was delighted. "That's it—that's it. Now tell how it is with us."
>
> George went on. "With us it ain't like that. We got a future. We got someone to talk to that gives a damn about us. We don't have to sit in no bar room blown' in our jack jus' because we got no place else to go. If them other guys gets in jail they can rot for all anybody gives a damn. But not us."
>
> Lennie broke in. *"But not us! An' why? Because ... because I got you to look after me, and you got me to look after you, and that's why."* He laughed delightedly. "Go on now, George!"[2]

---

[1] John Steinbeck, *Of Mice and Men* (New York: Penguin Books, 1993), p. 2.
[2] Ibid., pp. 13–14 (emphasis in original).

In a world as isolated and broken as ours, there's power in having a friend who genuinely says, "I got you to look after me, and you got me to look after you." If we learned anything during the initial outbreak of the coronavirus, it was just how essential relationships are to human flourishing. Will we ever again shut down economies, lock down families, and separate people from each other quite so eagerly? The devastating psychological effects will take years to grasp fully. In the words of another character in *Of Mice and Men*, "A guy goes nuts if he ain't got anybody. Don't make any difference who the guy is, long's he's with you."[3] It goes without saying that we need authentic friendships in life. We need each other. We can't find happiness and fulfillment without a profound sense of belonging to one another.

We've also heard it a thousand times: we'll never be any better than the average of our five best friends. Our friends are the biggest indicators of who we are and where we're going in life. At their best, they shape our character, inspire our dreams, and spur us on. At their worst, they turn us in on ourselves and hold us back from being fully human and fully ourselves.

From a Christian perspective, we can go one step further and acknowledge the power of Christ-centered friendship to help us pursue God's will for our lives. If you look down the long line of saints throughout human history, they banded together with like-minded friends, pushing one another to ever greater heights of virtue, prayer, and mission.

Take a look around you. Which of your friends have the biggest influence on who you're becoming right now? Are they circumstantial or intentional friendships? Do they inspire you to pursue excellence and chase after noble dreams?

[3] Ibid., pp. 72–73.

One of the main reasons I kept the faith in college was that I saw a profound joy and mutual trust among the Christians I met in the first few weeks of my freshman year. They were clearly living for something bigger than themselves. Their love for one another was not only deep but also devoid of expectations and pressure. They simply loved each other for who they were. Around the same time, I picked up *Mere Christianity* by C. S. Lewis for the first time and realized why I was so inspired by these friends. They embodied Lewis' description of the "new men", those Christians whose lives were seized by the love of God and spilled over with love for others:

> Already the new men are dotted here and there all over the earth. Some, as I have admitted, are still hardly recognisable: but others can be recognised. Every now and then one meets them. Their very voices and faces are different from ours: stronger, quieter, happier, more radiant. They begin where most of us leave off. They are, I say, recognisable; but you must know what to look for. They will not be very like the idea of "religious people" which you have formed from your general reading. They do not draw attention to themselves. You tend to think that you are being kind to them when they are really being kind to you. They love you more than other men do, but they need you less.[4]

The fact that authentic friendship has become such a precious commodity is a point of historical significance. When was the last time you read a philosophically robust book on friendship? Why have we abdicated our standards of friendship to self-help authors and iconic sitcoms from the '90s? There's tremendous confusion in our world today

[4] C. S. Lewis, *Mere Christianity* (San Francisco: HarperSanFrancisco, 2001), p. 223.

about what it means to be in right relationship with each other. Our society has obsessed over self-determination and forgotten the power of self-donation. People don't know who they are and therefore don't know how to make a gift of themselves to others. There's no doubt that social media has watered down our notion of human connection, and very few of us have models of virtuous friendship to imitate. It's no wonder that loneliness is on the rise.

Over the last few decades, science has caught up to this great need we all have for friendship, declaring it critical for personal health, necessary for overcoming adversity, and helpful in increasing our overall attractiveness.[5] Whether convinced by theological truth, scientific discoveries, or basic common sense, nobody can live long without friends.

Most fundamentally, friendship opens us up to the gift of others. It reminds us that we're not alone in the world. It has the potential to bring out the best in us, remind us who we are, and keep us moving toward the highest ideals. Aristotle describes three levels of friendship: utility, pleasure, and excellence.[6] Each is important, and the strongest friendships often integrate all three.

THREE LEVELS OF FRIENDSHIP

Friendship of *utility* is born out of mutual benefit: housemates, classmates, teammates, colleagues. These are people you share life with out of convenience or circumstance.

---

[5] Beth Dreher, "10 Facts That Prove Friends Are Ridiculously Healthy for Us", *The Healthy*, August 27, 2020, https://www.thehealthy.com/family /relationships/friends-facts/.

[6] Aristotle, *Nicomachean Ethics* VIII, trans. W.D. Ross, from the Internet Classics Archive, 1994–2009, http://classics.mit.edu/Aristotle/nicomachaen .8.viii.html.

They're useful to you, which doesn't mean that you're using them but simply appreciating the practical purpose they serve. Consider your first friend in high school, likely someone you sat next to in class or lined up next to on the sports field. Consider your coworkers or the people next to you on the bus every day. Consider your neighbors. There's nothing wrong with convenience or utility. It's where most friendships begin.

As you come to know yourself more deeply, you long for friends who share your interests and make you happy. These are friendships of *pleasure*. They are the easy and life-giving people in your life whom you simply enjoy being around. They likely share your outlook on life and enjoy pursuing the same hobbies. When you're with them, you laugh easily and rest in their presence. These friendships satisfy your need to belong to others, to enjoy a shared life. In the words of C. S. Lewis in *The Four Loves*, "Friendship is the least jealous of loves. Two friends delight to be joined by a third, and three by a fourth."[7] To take genuine pleasure in other people as friends is one of the most natural forms of human relationship. They bring out something unique in us, just as we do in them. But if they become an obsession or an idol, the friendship quickly self-destructs. Like any pleasure in life, friendship must mature if it's going to endure.

Aristotle's highest form of friendship involves a common pursuit of excellence and *virtue*. It's the shared pursuit of not only a common goal but also the common good. Friendship of excellence is how we learn to share the greatest joys and struggles of our interior life. It's where we hold each other accountable in our pursuit of greatness. In the words of Lewis again, our first encounter with virtuous friends typically starts with something like, "What? You

---

[7] C. S. Lewis, *The Four Loves* (San Diego: Harcourt, 1960), p. 61.

too? I thought I was the only one."[8] We not only admire
the virtue we see in them, but we also help them strive for
it. We're willing to fight for their good even to the sacrifice of our own. This is ideal friendship, and most people
don't long for it, because they've never experienced it.

In his national bestseller *The Boys in the Boat*, author
Daniel James Brown tells the story of nine working-class
Americans and their historic journey to the 1936 Olympics in Berlin. They go on to win gold as an eight-oar
crew, but much of their success can be traced back to the
friendships that formed in their early years at the University of Washington. George Pocock, who single-handedly
designed and built the racing shells that won gold in mul-
tiple Olympics, was close to many of the coaches and
rowers from Washington. Brown summarizes Pocock's
observations of the most successful crews:

> He detected the strength of the gossamer threads of affec-
> tion that sometimes grew between a pair of young men
> or among a boatload of them striving honestly to do their
> best. And he came to understand how those almost mysti-
> cal bonds of trust and affection, if nurtured correctly, might
> lift a crew above the ordinary sphere, transport it to a place
> where nine boys somehow became one thing—a thing
> that could not quite be defined, a thing that was so in tune
> with the water and the earth and the sky above that, as they
> rowed, effort was replaced by ecstasy. It was a rare thing, a
> sacred thing, a thing devoutly to be hoped for.[9]

Perhaps we've all experienced similar "bonds of trust and
affection" throughout our lives, if not for long stretches of
time then at least in specific moments. My mind immediately goes to experiences on the sports field, group

---

[8] Ibid., p. 65.
[9] Daniel James Brown, *The Boys in the Boat* (New York: Penguin Books,
2013), p. 48.

projects in school, and countless friends who helped me launch missionary and entrepreneurial projects. All these endeavors required great friendships rooted in trust and shared goals that were infinitely bigger than any one man's dreams. From pro-life music festivals to intentional homes of community for young adults, all my greatest dreams have always been utterly dependent on virtuous friends. None of them would have been possible in isolation.

So why the lack of virtuous friendship in society today? In summary, there are a lot of lonely people out there afraid to make the first move. There's also a lot of fear keeping people from standing up for what is true, good, and beautiful. We must be bold and intentional. We must make the most of our friendships of utility and pleasure but always strive for more. Where are those people we can stand close to who are chasing after the highest ideals? How can we go about initiating friendship with people who are more virtuous than we are? When we do so, we allow their goodness to spill over into ours.

Ancient wisdom sums it up simply: "A faithful friend is a sturdy shelter: he that has found one has found a treasure. There is nothing so precious as a faithful friend, and no scales can measure his excellence. A faithful friend is an elixir of life; and those who fear the Lord will find him" (Sir 6:14–16). How easily we forget the power of faithful friends whose lives are oriented toward heaven. By the grace of God, they'll be the same souls we stand shoulder to shoulder with for all of eternity.

SOCIETY OF SAINTS

Two thousand years ago, the God of the universe lowered himself to the level of his disciples and said, "No longer do I call you servants.... I have called you friends" (Jn 15:15). Surely we can do the same. Surely we can step out of ourselves long enough to recognize our need for deep friendship, not only with others but ultimately with God. We are all capable of cultivating friendship that rises above convenience and pleasure, that soars to the heights of virtue and taps into our capacity for greatness.

According to Saint Thomas Aquinas, friendliness is a virtue. He describes it as a habit of "both deeds and words" that enables us to "behave towards one another in a becoming manner".[10] It's my favorite of all the natural virtues because it's not complicated. As long as we're rooted in God's love for us and have an authentic love for others, we cannot help but exude likability and trust. We become the kind of person with whom others want to be friends. This virtue of affability is shared by many of the greatest saints in heaven. Long before they were perfect, they were likable. They were loving. They engaged in friendship with others out of deep gratitude for the friendship that God had first shown them.

In the Church's official declaration on the heroic virtues of Blessed Álvaro del Portillo (immediate successor to Saint Josemaría Escrivá as the head of Opus Dei), Álvaro is described as "a man of profound goodness and affability, able to transmit peace and serenity to souls".[11] What a beautiful summary of a man's life, to be known for his goodness and friendliness so clearly rooted in the Lord. Similarly, one of the great gifts of Blessed Pier Giorgio Frassati was his ability to make friends. He was a prankster

---

[10] Aquinas, *Summa Theologiae* II-II, q. 114, art. 1.

[11] Wlodimierz Redzioch, "Interview with Inside the Vatican (October 8, 2014)", *Romana: Bulletin of the Prelature of the Holy Cross and Opus Dei*, no. 59 (July–December 2014): 319–21, https://en.romana.org/59/articles-and-inter views/interview-with-inside-the-vatican-october-8-2014/.

and an adventurer. He was always happy to see two friends become three and three become four. Whether he was leading his friends on a Saturday morning hike or caring for the poor in the streets of Turin, he had mastered the virtue of affability by the time he died of polio at the age of twenty-four. Similarly, I can't help but reflect on the uproarious life of G. K. Chesterton. If his cause for canonization is ever opened, Chesterton's heroic virtues will include his mirth and magnetic personality. By drawing others to himself through his unabashed friendliness, Chesterton drew countless souls to God.

Ultimately, to love others is to love their souls, to want eternal life for them. The greatest pursuit of excellence always mirrors the friendships of the saints. In the explanatory notes of the old Roman Missal (1962), the Church describes "one of the joys of eternal salvation" as the "ravishing society of all the other citizens of heaven" who are even now interceding on our behalf.[12] In defiance of the world, the flesh, and the devil, it is the saints who stand shoulder to shoulder in pursuit of God. They are a mystery to others and often a mystery to themselves. Like them, we can learn how to love the world passionately without a hint of attachment to it. We too can captivate the world with the precious and rare gift of authentic friendship.

Let's return briefly to the near-closing words of C. S. Lewis in his masterpiece of apologetics *Mere Christianity*. As he concludes what began as a radio series that saved countless souls from the pitfalls of atheism during World War II, he completes his description of the "new men", those scattered but faithful Christians across the world:

---

[12] *Roman Catholic Daily Missal, 1962* (Kansas City, MO: Angelus Press, 2004), p. 899.

They will usually seem to have a lot of time: you will wonder where it comes from. When you have recognised one of them, you will recognise the next one much more easily. And I strongly suspect (but how should I know?) that they recognise one another immediately and infallibly, across every barrier of colour, sex, class, age, and even of creeds. In that way, to become holy is rather like joining a secret society. To put it at the very lowest, it must be great *fun*.[13]

Indeed, I cannot imagine anything more fun, anything more practical, anything more revolutionary than a secret society of aspiring saints. There's nothing complicated about embracing this *apostolate of friendship* as our own. We begin by entering into deep and joyful friendship with fellow disciples of our Lord Jesus Christ. We spur each other on to become great lovers of God. We band together with the saints who constantly remind us that our citizenship is in heaven. Then, we go out in pursuit of souls by offering them one of the greatest gifts this side of heaven: authentic friendship. There's no more natural way to spread the Gospel and invite others into eternal friendship with God.

As I mentioned previously, my three friends and I who went on pilgrimage together ten years ago are still very close. I'm the only one not on track to become a priest, but the Lord remains the foundation for our continued and ever-deepening friendship. Only he can unite us across hundreds of miles of distance. Only he can inspire such a deep and meaningful brotherhood that constantly runs deeper and aims higher. These men have taught me time and time again what it means to be human and how to valiantly evangelize our culture fraught with relativism

---

[13] Lewis, *Mere Christianity*, p. 223 (emphasis in original).

and noise. I cannot imagine the last decade of life without them.

How, then, do we take this principle to the next level and cultivate friendship with God? What does it look like to be so rooted in him that everything else follows suit, including our most important relationships? The answer brings us to our next principle in the art of being human: *prayer.*

GETTING PRACTICAL

- Do a quick analysis of your top five friends. How many of these friendships are based in utility or pleasure? Are any of them rooted in excellence or virtue?
- Build virtuous friendship with people of the same sex. If you find this difficult, go on a dating fast to clear your head and purify your intentions.
- Call an old friend once a month without an agenda. Simply delight in his existence. If you're reminded of a shared pursuit of excellence, thank your friend for spurring you on.
- Find an example of virtuous friendship in history, and model one of your friendships after it.
- Explore the connection between friendship and the previous principles of wonder and freedom. Ponder its connection to forthcoming principles like prayer and community.

FURTHER READING

Aelred of Rievaulx. *Spiritual Friendship.* Translated by M. Eugenia Laker. Notre Dame, IN: Ave Maria Press, 2008.

Ahern, Patrick. *Maurice and Thérèse: The Story of a Love.* New York: Doubleday, 1998.

Aristotle. *Nicomachean Ethics* VIII. Translated by W.D. Ross. From the Internet Classics Archive, 1994–2009. http://classics.mit.edu/Aristotle/nicomachaen.8.viii .html.

Cuddeback, John. *True Friendship: Where Virtue Becomes Happiness*. San Francisco: Ignatius Press, 2021.

Lewis, C.S. *The Four Loves*. San Diego: Harcourt, 1960.

Chapter 4

Prayer

prer | *noun* | *a solemn request for help or expression of thanks addressed to God.*

Nothing could have prepared me for the Ironman of pilgrimages known as Lough Derg. No state championship football team. No Olympic training. No thirty-day silent retreat. To this day, nothing has come close to the spiritual, physical, and mental intensity that awaited me at this ancient pilgrimage site on Station Island in County Donegal, Ireland.

Legend has it that Lough Derg was a destination for Christians dating all the way back to the time of Saint Patrick, after Christ revealed to him a cave-like entrance to Purgatory on the island.[1] I arrived there fifteen hundred years later with a few of my closest friends, expecting something like a memorable weekend retreat. It was August 2016, and the sun was nowhere in sight. There was a surprisingly cold breeze and persistent rain. Within the first few minutes of our boat ride to the island, our guide informed us that we weren't going to sleep for the next forty hours. Nor were we going to eat more than one meal a day (consisting of dry toast and coffee). To top

[1] Ludwig Bieler, "St. Patrick's Purgatory: Contributions towards an Historical Topography", *Irish Ecclesiastical Record* 93, series 5 (1960): 137–44.

it off, we were the last to arrive on the island and already running behind on the 1,413 Hail Marys, 846 Our Fathers, and 270 Apostles' Creeds that we would pray over the next three days. Our guide then told us to take off our shoes (we wouldn't need them anymore) and get started. I laughed nervously and thought to myself, *Only the Irish could come up with a penance like this and call it a pilgrimage.* Given the island's many intimidating nicknames, I shouldn't have been surprised.

During the first few hours of the pilgrimage, I noticed that my prayers and mortifications were slowly building off each other. The more I prayed and fasted, the more open I became to God's will. One of the most intense parts of the repeated prayer stations included going to a cross on the outside wall of the island's basilica, kneeling to say a few prayers, and then standing with arms fully outstretched toward the sea, saying three times, "I renounce the world, the flesh, and the devil." It was totally unforgettable. This first forty-hour vigil dedicated to nonstop prayer was at the heart of the pilgrimage. Only occasionally, we'd take a break to warm up with Lough Derg soup, which consisted of hot boiling water and endless supplies of salt and pepper.

As we progressed through these prayer stations, which meant the frequent kneeling on penitential prayer beds made of remnants from the original monastery, the ebb and flow of the pilgrimage slowly expanded my receptivity to God's grace. In times of quiet reflection, I found an honesty and a humility that had been missing from my life for quite some time. On the final day, after making a good confession and getting a solid night of sleep, I walked into the basilica for the closing Mass. I noticed a beautiful plaque near the entrance that read, "I am the door, enter and be safe." It was a paraphrase from the Gospel of John: "I am the door; if any one enters by me,

he will be saved, and will go in and out and find pasture"
(10:9). Immediately, my eyes welled up with tears. I was
suddenly struck by God's protection and providence over
my whole life up until that point. For a moment, I could
see all the twists and turns he had carried me through and
all the ups and downs he had used for his greater glory. I
could see all the ways he had forgiven me and even protected me from sin. In that moment, I was overwhelmed
by his goodness and faithfulness as a Father, how he had
never given up on me nor ever stopped loving me. It was
an extraordinary grace that culminated with Holy Communion about thirty minutes later.

Like any good retreat or prayer, a pilgrimage is an opportunity to abandon ourselves to God and to see ourselves in
the light of his love. Because of the built-in discomfort and
difficulty of Lough Derg, it had a way of expediting the
process. It brought sins, wounds, and struggles to the surface of my soul. It was like Lent intensified into a three-day
experience that made it easier to surrender burdens, seek
healing, and find detachment. While most people won't
have the opportunity to experience Lough Derg during
their lives, no one is held back from the opportunity to
enter into the fire of God's love every day in prayer.

BEYOND THE HERE AND NOW

What exactly is prayer? It's the lifting of one's heart to
God, often called the prelude to eternal life. Our soul needs
prayer as our lungs need oxygen. It's the highest form of
leisure, which is our fifth principle. It's the force undergird-
ing all our best *work*, which is our sixth principle. It reveals
the deepest seat of our soul, where we come to know God
as both infinite Creator and intimate Friend. In prayer, he

dares to come close. He invites us to share in his divine nature. Therefore, praying in spirit and truth means allowing the Holy Spirit to groan within us, teaching us how to rejoice in our identity as beloved children and to unite our sacrifice of praise with that of Jesus Christ. It's easier said than done, especially in a culture that has digressed from basic beliefs in God's existence and loving providence.

A few years ago at the MTV Awards, actor Chris Pratt took everyone by surprise as he received the Generation Award and boldly proclaimed the immortality of the soul and the importance of prayer. In between hilarious and awkward words of advice, he offered several rules for life that could have easily come out of a catechism:

> Number 2: You have a soul. Be careful with it....
> Number 6: God is real. God loves you. God wants the best for you. Believe that. I do....
> Number 8: Learn to pray. It's easy, and it's so good for your soul. And finally, number 9: Nobody is perfect. People are going to tell you, "You're perfect just the way you are." You're not! You are imperfect. You always will be. But, there is a powerful force that designed you that way. And if you're willing to accept that, you will have grace. And grace is a gift. And like the freedom that we enjoy in this country, that grace was paid for with somebody else's blood. Do not forget it. Don't take it for granted.[2]

In a world that has left God behind, these are gutsy remarks. In a post-Christian culture, the very idea that human beings have immortal souls is revolutionary. Rare are the corporate, political, and even religious leaders who teach us to look beyond the here and now. Rare are the

---

[2] Christopher Michael Pratt, *2018 MTV Video Music Awards* (Radio City Music Hall, New York City, August 20, 2018).

friends and mentors who teach us how to take care of our souls. Yet, isn't there something in all of us that knows we'll live forever? Isn't there a touch of the infinite in every human heart that points to eternity, that reminds us we're not home yet? That's why Pratt's speech was so powerful. He tapped into the most innate but overlooked desires of the human heart.

If not for the grace of God, how easily we would go through our entire lives without pondering anything beyond our senses. If we can't see it, hear it, or touch it, we often don't stop to contemplate it. Some would call this rationalism gone wild. In his semi-autobiographical masterpiece *Orthodoxy*, Chesterton calls it plain old materialism with an embarrassing lack of imagination:

> Mr. McCabe thinks me a slave because I am not allowed to believe in determinism. I think Mr. McCabe a slave because he is not allowed to believe in fairies. But if we examine the two vetoes we shall see that his is really much more of a pure veto than mine. The Christian is quite free to believe that there is a considerable amount of settled order and inevitable development in the universe. But the materialist is not allowed to admit into his spotless machine the slightest speck of spiritualism or miracle. Poor Mr. McCabe is not allowed to retain even the tiniest imp, though it might be hiding in a pimpernel.[3]

To be human is to have a body endowed with an immortal soul, to see beyond the physical into the spiritual realm. Through prayer, we become aware of this spiritual realm. We enter into friendship with the Lord Jesus Christ and cultivate our lifelong discipleship with him. As prayer purifies and elevates our souls, the Holy Spirit helps us to

[3] G. K. Chesterton, *Orthodoxy* (Nashville: Love Good, 2017), p. 26.

see as God sees and to love as God loves. Consistent prayer gives us a peace beyond all understanding and reminds us of the most important truth of all: we are infinitely loved. If we settle for anything less, we'll miss out on the greatest truths and miracles of the human experience.

There are many forms of prayer, but all of them fall under one of four categories: thanksgiving, praise, petition, and intercession. First, *thanksgiving* refers to any moment in which we lift our hearts to God and thank him for all the good things he has done for us. Because joy is the overflow of a grateful heart, prayers of thanksgiving are vital for any Christian seeking to spread the joy of the Gospel. Second, *praise* is adoration and worship of God for his sheer goodness. It's a great way to begin prayer, by simply giving God glory for who he is. It's also at the heart of worship, the highest form of prayer. Third, *petition* is asking God for things that we need, whether they're specific graces or full-blown miracles. Petition is the most common form of prayer when we're young. When it comes to petitioning God, the more bold and specific we are the better. Finally, *intercession* covers all the prayers that we lift up on behalf of others. Whether praying for a grandmother with cancer or for the conversion of a friend, there are graces that God specifically distributes through intercessory prayers. Their power cannot be overestimated.

Regardless of whether we more often turn to thanksgiving, praise, petition, or intercession in our daily prayers, all of them point to God and remind us who we are as beloved sons and daughters. Through prayer, the Church teaches us that Christ reveals "the mystery of the Father and his love" and "fully reveals man to man himself".[4]

---

[4] Second Vatican Council, Pastoral Constitution on the Church in the Modern Word *Gaudium et Spes* (December 7, 1965), no. 22, https://www.vatican.va/archive/hist_councils/ii_vatican_council/documents/vat-ii_cons_19651207_gaudium-et-spes_en.html.

We were not able to know ourselves till Christ came.

Through prayer, God bestows and confirms our identity. We belong to him, and prayer is how he ensures that we never forget it.

PRAYING WITH THE CHURCH

What does it look like to pray with discipline and desire? To be consistent in prayer without it becoming routine, without losing the fire of divine love? God is the great Lover of our souls and the fulfillment of all our desires. He thirsts for us beyond our wildest imagination, and prayer is our childlike response to his great love. To pray like a child is to pray with loving abandonment, a spirit of adventure, radical presence in the moment, and joyful dependency on God. It's an act of justice by which we give God his due as Creator and Savior. Saint John Henry Newman's great motto captures the essence of prayer: *cor ad cor loquitur*, or "heart speaks unto heart." Through prayer, the heart of God speaks to the heart of man. Over time and with the help of God's grace, prayer gives us a divine perspective on everything. Eternity touches down in our souls. Again, we learn to see as God sees and love as God loves.

Since the beginning of Christendom, the Lord has blessed the Church with mystics, saints, and martyrs who have taught us how to pray with the heart of a child. We can stand on their shoulders and press into the Church's own rhythm of prayer. The Church is in every way our Mother and always the one best suited to teach us how to pray:

> The Tradition of the Church proposes to the faithful certain rhythms of praying intended to nourish continual prayer. Some are daily, such as morning and evening prayer, grace before and after meals, the Liturgy of the Hours. Sundays,

centered on the Eucharist, are kept holy primarily by prayer. The cycle of the liturgical year and its great feasts are also basic rhythms of the Christian's life of prayer.[5]

For Catholics, the highest form of prayer is the Holy Sacrifice of the Mass. Encountering the Lord Jesus Christ in the Eucharist and partaking in his once and eternal sacrifice at Calvary is foundational to every other kind of prayer. In the most tangible yet mysterious way, heaven touches down and kisses earth at every Mass. At no other moment during our earthly lives will we be closer to God and to the rest of the Mystical Body of Christ. Receiving Holy Communion at Mass prepares us for heaven, putting the rest of our lives in perspective and deepening our longing for eternal glory.

Out of the Mass flows the Liturgy of the Hours. This universal prayer of the Church is rooted in ancient Jewish practices and dates all the way back to the time of Saint Benedict fifteen hundred years ago. It's a rhythmic way of praying through the Scriptures, with particular focus on the Psalms alongside various readings from the Old and New Testaments. What better way to develop a deep love for the Word of God and punctuate our day with moments of profound recollection? It also unites us with the universal Church throughout the world as millions of priests, religious, and laypeople pray it across every time zone.

Similarly transformative, Adoration of the Blessed Sacrament allows our souls to be refreshed by the intimacy of divine love. It's an extension of the Consecration at Mass whereby we behold Jesus Christ in the Blessed Sacrament and allow him to behold us. In the silence and stillness of Adoration, we come to know that God is God and we are

---

[5] *Catechism of the Catholic Church*, no. 2698.

not. We realize the depths of love from which we came and the heights of love for which we are destined.

Popularized at a similar time in Church history, the Rosary has pride of place in the Church's long history of devotions. With the help of the Blessed Mother's intercession, the Rosary calls to mind the life, death, and Resurrection of our Lord Jesus Christ. Long before literacy was widespread or Scripture widely available due to the printing press, the faith was learned and passed on to future generations through the Rosary. Just as powerfully now as then, the Rosary encompasses all the key mysteries of our faith.

For those who are Catholic, the Sacrament of Reconciliation on a regular basis is the fast track to deepening our intimacy with God. We're not only forgiven of our sins after every good confession, but we are also delivered from them. In this regard, growth in the spiritual life has less to do with perfectionism and everything to do with how quickly and how deeply we trust in God's mercy after every fall.

Alongside these liturgical, devotional, and vocal prayers that require so much humility and trust in the Church, it's vital that we engage daily in mental prayer. Distinct from traditional or memorized prayers, mental prayer refers to our personal conversation with God. It's how we pray when we speak to him as a friend. Because I'm easily distracted, my best mental prayer often takes the form of spiritual journaling. I write everything down that I'm saying to God, and then I listen. I've never heard his voice come out of the clouds, but I often sense him responding to me in the interior of my heart. So I leave a space in my journal, and then I put in brackets what I hear God saying in response. It's often a blend of Scripture passages that I've recently read.

According to Saint Alphonsus de Liguori, nothing more powerfully combats sin than mental prayer:

> Some say many vocal prayers; but he who does not make mental prayer will scarcely say his vocal prayers with attention: he will say them with distractions, and the Lord will not hear him. "Many cry to God," says St. Augustine, "but not with the voice of the soul, but with the voice of the body; only the cry of the heart, of the soul, reaches God." It is not enough to pray only with the tongue: we must, according to the Apostle, pray also with the heart if we wish to receive God's graces: *Praying at all times in the Spirit.* And by experience we see that many persons who recite a great number of vocal prayers, the Office and the Rosary, fall into sin, and continue to live in sin. But he who attends to mental prayer scarcely ever falls into sin.[6]

He goes on to write that "all the saints have become saints by mental prayer."[7] Therefore, personal prayer from the heart is an indispensable aspect of the Christian life. We must speak to God as a Father and know him as a Friend. We must learn how to listen, always falling back on the Word of God if we struggle to hear the voice of God. Saint Teresa of Ávila powerfully admonishes:

> If you do not practice mental prayer, you don't need any devil to throw you into hell, you throw yourself in there of your own accord. On the contrary, give me the greatest of all sinners; if he practices mental prayer, be it only for fifteen minutes every day, he will be converted.[8]

---

[6] Alphonsus de Liguori, *Dignity and Duties of the Priest*, ed. Eugene Grimm (Brooklyn, NY: Redemptorist Fathers, 1927), p. 292 (emphasis in original).

[7] Ibid.

[8] Cited in Jean-Baptiste Chautard, O.C.S.O., *The Soul of the Apostolate*, trans. a monk of Our Lady of Gethsemani (Trappist, KY: Abbey of Gethsemani, 1946), p. 82.

Fifteen to thirty minutes of loving dialogue with our Maker
and Redeemer every day is a nonnegotiable discipline for
the aspiring saint. On top of cultivating the full depths of
our humanity, nothing more powerfully assists our Lord
in the salvation of souls. He wants us praying on our knees
long before he wants us preaching on street corners. To be
great missionaries, we must first be great mystics.

Once we're praying with the heart of a child and with
the heart of the Church, we begin to pray without ceasing.
We still need key moments set aside every day for uninter-
rupted prayer, but a ceaseless prayer of the heart can become
habitual. Daily silence and intermittent fasting also go a
long way toward advancing a spirit of prayer in our souls.
Spontaneous aspirations, especially little interior bursts of
memorized Scripture, allow for countless moments of grace
throughout the day. Additionally, true devotion to Mary
is a quick way toward all growth in the spiritual life. She is
the staircase by which our Lord descended from heaven
into history, and she remains the staircase by which we
climb to the heights of holiness. Total consecration to our
Lady with the help of Saint Louis Marie de Montfort has
transformed my life time and time again.[9]

PRAYER WITHOUT CEASING

It was the spring of 2008, and I was weeks away from my
college graduation. A handful of us ventured to Washington, DC, and New York City to see Pope Benedict XVI
on his American tour. The entire week felt like a collision
of worlds: everything I loved about being Catholic coming
together with everything I loved about being American.

[9] Louis-Marie de Montfort, *True Devotion to the Blessed Virgin Mary* (Rock-
ford, IL: Tan Books, 1941).

One of the most iconic moments occurred watching the Holy Father on television as he ate cake and celebrated his eighty-first birthday at the White House. His smile that day captured so much of the deep joy I felt while he was in the country. When he left a few days later, he took a piece of my heart with him.

On one of the final days of his American tour, he arrived by helicopter at a massive field in Yonkers, where tens of thousands of young people were gathered in anticipation. My friends and I had arrived eight hours earlier to be in the front row and enjoy the "pre-game" entertainment featuring everyone from Matt Maher to Kelly Clarkson. During the climax of his electric speech that day, Pope Benedict powerfully proclaimed:

> What matters most is that you develop your personal relationship with God. That relationship is expressed in prayer. God by his very nature speaks, hears, and replies. Indeed, Saint Paul reminds us: we can and should "pray constantly" (1 Thess 5:17). Far from turning in on ourselves or withdrawing from the ups and downs of life, by praying we turn towards God and through him to each other, including the marginalized and those following ways other than God's path (cf. *Spe Salvi*, 33). As the saints teach us so vividly, prayer becomes hope in action. Christ was their constant companion, with whom they conversed at every step of their journey for others.[10]

For me, that moment confirmed the most simple and profound truth of the Christian life: *Nothing* matters more than intimacy with God. There is no greater joy in this

[10] Benedict XVI, Apostolic Journey to the United States of America and Visit to the United Nations Organization Headquarters: Meeting with Young People and Seminarians (address, Saint Joseph Seminary, Yonkers, NY, April 19, 2008), https://www.vatican.va/content/benedict-xvi/en/speeches/2008/april/documents/hf_ben-xvi_spe_20080419_st-joseph-seminary.html.

life than to be a companion of Christ. Through prayer, we enter into the sanctuary of our hearts to dialogue with the great Lover of our souls. Whether its regular disciplines like the Rosary or the silent contemplation that Pope Benedict XVI called for during that unforgettable speech, prayer is our nourishment and strength. It draws us into the depths of God's love. And there's no greater foundation for cultivating the art of being human.

Few have responded more radically to this call to constant prayer than Pope Benedict XVI's patron saint, Saint Benedict of Nursia. As the ancient Roman cultural order was collapsing around him in the sixth century, Saint Benedict fled Rome and spent three years praying in a cave. Eventually others joined him, giving rise to Western monasticism and much of Christian culture. In the centuries that followed, the Benedictine rhythm of prayer, work, and study spread the faith across Europe and built Western civilization as we know it.

What, then, is the role of prayer in making us more human and evangelizing our culture of noise? Do we believe that prayer is the most powerful foundation for the apostolic life? Do we pray daily, and if so, what does it look like? Whether your prayer life looks more like a weekend at Lough Derg or a contemplative escape into a cave, God is calling you deeper. He is calling you to be a great saint rooted in prayer. As Dom Jean-Baptiste Chautard reminds us in *The Soul of the Apostolate*, "Only the interior life can sustain us in the hidden, backbreaking labor of planting the seed that seems to go so long without fruit."[11] Those of us who are prone to activity must be especially committed to prayer above all else.

As we reflect on our previous principles of wonder, freedom, and friendship, let us commit ever more

---

[11] Chautard, *Soul of the Apostolate*, p. 153.

radically to the interior life that provides the only true and lasting foundation for the apostolic life. Without a deep commitment to this loving friendship with God, there's no chance we'll be fully human or fully alive—much less help Jesus save souls or rebuild Christian culture. Only through prayer will we become who God has created us to be and stay humble enough to do all things for his greater glory.

GETTING PRACTICAL

- Set aside a space in your home for prayer. It can be an entire room or simply one corner of your bedroom. Then, commit to solid vocal prayers every day at the same time in that space (Act of Faith, Chaplet of Divine Mercy, Rosary, etc.).
- Practice the heroic minute every day, dropping to your knees as soon as your alarm clock sounds to pray three Hail Marys and a Morning Offering.
- Commit to fifteen or thirty minutes of mental prayer every day. If you're struggling to listen, slowly read through the Psalms or one of the Gospels. Stop frequently, listen, and write inspirations down in a spiritual journal.
- If you're Catholic, start going to daily Mass more often, and make a habit of regular Confession.
- Commit to Adoration or significant spiritual reading once a week (see book recommendations below).
- Go on an annual silent retreat.

FURTHER READING

Boylan, Eugene. *This Tremendous Lover*. London: Baronius Press, 2019.

Garrigou-Lagrange, Reginald, O.P. *The Three Ages of the Interior Life: Prelude of Eternal Life*. Vol. 1. London: Catholic Way Publishing, 2014.

Oratio: Rhythms of Prayer from the Heart of the Church, Deluxe Edition. Edited by Jimmy Mitchell. Palm Harbor, FL: Love Good, 2022.

De Sales, Francis. *Introduction to the Devout Life*. Translated by John K. Ryan. New York: Doubleday, 2003.

Sarah, Robert Cardinal. *The Power of Silence: Against the Dictatorship of Noise*. Translated by Michael J. Miller. San Francisco: Ignatius Press, 2017.

Thérèse of Lisieux. *The Story of a Soul: The Autobiography of the Little Flower*. Edited by Mother Agnes of Jesus. Translated by Michael Day, Cong., Orat. Charlotte, NC: Saint Benedict Press, TAN Books, 2010.

Chapter 5

Leisure ᵢₙ𝒹ᵤₗᵧₑₙₜ

'lēZHǝr | noun | use of free time for enjoyment.

My first-ever cigar was a full-bodied Cuban, and smoking it with my best friend on a park bench in Antigua, Guatemala, was one of the most unforgettable experiences of my life. It led to conversation and contemplation about the mysteries of life, and it came right at the halfway point of a life-changing summer. We were living as missionaries in Honduras but had a week off to backpack through ancient Mayan ruins and volcanoes in Guatemala. As soon as we returned to Honduras, we continued coordinating the work, prayer, and formation of hundreds of Americans coming down for their annual mission trips.

I was twenty years old and previously hadn't been out of the country except once with my high school youth group and briefly another time on a cruise with my family. I had never smoked a cigar or even enjoyed my first alcoholic drink. My reasons were somewhat personal, given the history of lung cancer and alcoholism in my family, but I also had a naturally conservative bent when it came to morals and an achievement mentality that sometimes made it difficult to relax. I often lived as if nothing could get in the way of my pursuit of perfection and productivity.

After the first few weeks of missionary work that summer, I woke up to a far richer truth: that the happiest people are not those ~~who achieve~~ more success in life but who maximize their receptivity to God's love. As I smoked my first cigar and mused with my best friend that night, we agreed that joy was found not in worldly achievement but in embracing God's will with gratitude and joy. Much to our surprise, we were learning these eternal truths as missionaries from the orphaned children and abandoned mothers we were there to serve. They were showing us how to slow down, drink deeply of life, and rejoice in the little things. They were teaching us the art of true leisure.

The irony is that our society often associates *leisure* with those living in prosperity, not abject poverty. What could the poor possibly teach us about spending our free time well? They don't have access to symphonies or sporting events. They can't afford Cuban cigars or fancy vacations—and yet, the poorest of the poor seem happier than the rest of us. How is that possible? How can poverty and joy coexist so seamlessly?

I believe that the best explanation is found in poetry, which has a powerful way of communicating mystery and paradox. It rises above rational discourse and cuts to the heart. Having worked alongside artists in the music industry for more than ten years, I know its power in music. Great songwriting is inseparable from rhythm, rhyme, and imagery. Many years ago, a friend of mine began writing songs based on the poetry of Gerard Manley Hopkins, a great Jesuit who died in obscurity but whose genius was popularized years later by fellow poet Robert Bridges. Of all the masterful poems by Hopkins, my favorite remains *God's Grandeur*:

> The world is charged with the grandeur of God.
> It will flame out, like shining from shook foil;
> It gathers to a greatness, like the ooze of oil

Crushed. Why do men then now not reck his rod?
Generations have trod, have trod, have trod;
   And all is seared with trade; bleared, smeared
      with toil;
   And wears man's smudge and shares man's smell:
      the soil
Is bare now, nor can foot feel, being shod.
And for all this, nature is never spent;
   There lives the dearest freshness deep down
      things;
And though the last lights off the black West went
   Oh, morning, at the brown brink eastward,
      springs—
Because the Holy Ghost over the bent
   World broods with warm breast and with ah!
      bright wings.[1]

Do we need a master's degree in philosophy, English, or theology to experience a world charged with the grandeur of God? Do we need great wealth to live life in full color? While intellectual depth and economic security can certainly facilitate a life of leisure, childlike receptivity is what matters most. We must slow down and learn how to find God's glory hidden behind the thin veils of creation, love, and artistic beauty.

What exactly is leisure, then, and what does it have to teach us about being human and evangelizing culture?

BEING OVER DOING

We are not human *doings*. Though our world obsesses with accomplishment, we are fundamentally good because

[1] Gerard Manley Hopkins, *Poems of Gerard Manley Hopkins*, ed. Robert Bridges (London: Humphrey Milford, 1918), p. 26.

God spoke in Jesus Baptism — apart from
any action God said He was pleased
with him because

we exist. We're more than our productivity. Our identity runs deeper than the sum of our successes or failures. He ju
Leisure, though often misunderstood, is the principle that was
best reminds us of these life-giving truths. It has everything
to do with *prayer*, for its highest form is divine worship. It
necessarily precedes *work*, for "work is the means of life"
and "leisure the end" as the late Roger Scruton reminds
us.[2] It reminds us that we work for the sake of rest, not the
other way around.

It takes a long time in today's utilitarian culture to realize that our deepest identity has less to do with *doing* and
more to do with *being*. Leisure is rest, an interior stillness
that fights against noise and activism. It's not loafing. It's
not escapism. It's a posture that conditions us to encounter
truth, beauty, and goodness. It's a disposition of soul that
connects us with reality, reminding us that life is precious
and that our infinite desires will be stilled only in eternity.
Leisure battles against idleness as much as it battles against
workaholism, keeping our eyes fixed on the horizon with
our feet firmly planted on the ground. In his seminal work
Leisure: The Basis of Culture, German philosopher Josef
Pieper describes leisure as follows:

> Leisure is a form of that stillness that is necessary prepara-
> tion for accepting reality; only the person who is still can
> hear, and whoever is not still, cannot hear. Such stillness
> is not mere soundlessness or a dead muteness; it means,
> rather, that the soul's power, as real, of responding to the
> real ... has not yet descended into words. Leisure is the dis-
> position of perceptive understanding, of contemplative
> beholding, and immersion—in the real.[3]

[2] Roger Scruton, Introduction to *Leisure: The Basis of Culture* by Josef Pieper
(San Francisco: Ignatius Press, 2007), p. 60.
[3] Pieper, *Leisure*, p. 60.

Healthy leisure leads us to God
unhealthy - disconnects us from reality.
LEISURE 89

Leisure is about reality, about living *in the real*. It goes without saying that it has many enemies in our culture of noise: unbridled technology, scientism, sloth, and addiction, to name a few. As an example, technology can greatly improve society and help us forge the future, but our world has a blind trust in it. Rarely do we question its role in medicine, business, or education. We simply assume that "because we can, we should." Without authentic leisure keeping us connected to reality, we forget our inherent dignity. We forget that we're not just cogs in a wheel made for efficiency and comfort alone.

Imagine what it would feel like to have a healthy detachment from technology and work. Imagine punctuating your busiest days with intentional leisure. Imagine honoring your Sabbath rest without compromise. If you're anything like me, you sometimes work yourself into such exhaustion that your defenses against temptation come down. Rather than entering into leisure that gives you true rest, you settle for passing pleasures that lead only to sin, burnout, or despair. Too much mindless entertainment—or worse, abusive entertainment like pornography—leads to restlessness. It makes it impossible for our souls to be at ease. True leisure is the only way to bring about the interior restoration that we need, but this stands in stark contrast to our culture's norms of endless work and pleasure-seeking.

CULTIVATING LEISURE

One of the easiest ways to cultivate leisure in your daily life is to listen to music, read books, and enjoy art that reflect reality and lift your soul toward God. Beautiful music, books, and art have always been some of the greatest expressions of culture throughout human history. They don't have to be explicitly Christian to foster a spirit of leisure or dispose your soul to virtue. They simply need to be rooted in truth and beauty in order to transform your heart to love what is good. The best way to curate art and entertainment is first to reject everything counterfeit, evil, and ugly. If it glorifies or normalizes sin, it is a waste of your time. Then, actively discern what songs, stories, and images best orient your soul toward virtue. Do they inspire integrity, heroism, and self-sacrifice? Do they make it easier to love others without counting the costs? Do they lead to edifying conversations and spontaneous prayer? If so, then you can rest assured that they are well worth your time.

Dana Gioia, former chairman of the National Endowment for the Arts, describes the purpose of art as follows:

> The cynicism that pervades contemporary cultural life must be replaced by a deep confidence in the human purposes and importance of art. Art is not an elitist luxury or a game for intellectual coteries. It is a necessary component of human development, both individually and communally. Art educates our emotions and imagination. It awakens, enlarges, and refines our humanity. Remove it, dilute it, or pervert it, and a community or a nation suffers—becoming less compassionate, curious, and alert, more coarse, narrow, and self-satisfied.[4]

Without good art bringing us out of ourselves, it's only a matter of time before our souls shrivel and our culture implodes. This is particularly true for those who live in cities and have less access to the beauty of God's creation, for nature also has a powerful way of keeping us rooted in reality.

[4] Dana Gioia, "The Catholic Writer Today", *First Things*, December 2013, p. 41.

Similarly vital is a commitment to intellectual leisure. Rightly pursued, it gives us the mind of Christ, who is the source and summit of all truth. With the growing intellectual dishonesty of mainstream media and the eroding credibility of higher education, there's a great need to raise up a generation of truth seekers. What does it look like to think with the mind of Christ? How do we study wisdom for its own sake and posture ourselves to receive better the gift of contemplation? Lest we be "led away by diverse and strange teachings" (Heb 13:9), we need the philosophical formation that only the Church can provide in order to do this well.

In the same way that children play with more confidence and vitality when their playground has a solid boundary around it, the Church is the solid boundary within which the faithful wander and play.[5] Since she is first and foremost a Mother, the Church educates her children in the truth and protects us from the wiles of our enemies. Without her teachings, we are left to create our own creeds and be our own feeble authority. It's a great consolation to know that the Church has been in the business of developing doctrine and shepherding her flock for two thousand years. We're anything but alone in our discipline of intellectual leisure.

In *Orthodoxy*, Chesterton describes the pursuit of truth as a wild and "whirling adventure" that puts all heresies and counterfeits to rest:

> It is always simple to fall; there are an infinity of angles at which one falls, only one at which one stands. To have fallen into any one of the fads from Gnosticism to Christian Science would indeed have been obvious and tame. But to have avoided them all has been one whirling

[5] American Society of Landscape Architects, "ASLA 2006 Student Awards", https://www.asla.org/awards/2006/studentawards/282.html.

adventure; and in my vision the heavenly chariot flies thundering through the ages, the dull heresies sprawling and prostrate, the wild truth reeling but erect.[6]

In an age dictated by relativism, it's easy to lose our hunger for knowledge and objective reality. It doesn't take much to be distracted and deceived by the world's noise. Modern education doesn't help either, with its frequent focus on empiricism, materialism, and career preparation. In contrast, cultivating the life of the mind makes us more human and more fully alive. It's an act of authentic leisure that enables us to invite others more deeply into the truth. To think with the mind of Christ and the Church is true freedom, and we have a responsibility to share it with others.

You don't have to be a creative genius to raise your standard for music, books, and entertainment. Nor do you have to be a towering academic to commit to fifteen minutes of intellectual leisure every day. Both are accessible to anyone willing to be intentional with his free time and actively dispose his soul to virtue.

FROM ADVENTURE INTO WORSHIP

All in all, my favorite forms of leisure always involve adventure. Whether skiing in Colorado or exploring caves in Kentucky, these experiences always bring me out of myself and remind me that I belong to God. In the words of Saint John Paul II, "Life with Christ is a wonderful adventure. He alone can give full meaning to life, he alone is the centre of history. Live by him!"[7] On a related note,

[6] G. K. Chesterton, *Orthodoxy* (Nashville: Love Good, 2017), p. 126.

[7] John Paul II, Apostolic Journey to the Czech Republic: Mass for the Youth (homily, April 26, 1997), no. 8, https://www.vatican.va/content/john-paul-ii/en/homilies/1997/documents/hf_jp-ii_hom_19970426.html.

I have learned over time that my interior life is the greatest adventure of all. That's why prayer, and more specifically worship, is the highest form of leisure. It's a constant
reminder that the same God who breathes the stars into
existence breathes us into existence. He sustains us even
now with his love.

While living in Honduras as a missionary that summer
many years ago, I sent home weekly emails to family and
friends who wanted to stay in touch and hear how I was
doing. These messages eventually turned into a blog while
I studied abroad in Europe the following fall. I didn't
know the writings of Josef Pieper or Joseph Ratzinger yet,
but the idea of leisure was already solidifying itself in my
mind. Below is an excerpt from my last email that went
out that summer:

> America is a blessed society, at times crazed, but undeniably
> blessed. We claim diversity, freedom, and personal liberty.
> As "leaders of the free world," we pave the way for techno-
> logical advancement and increased effectiveness/efficiency
> in most if not all industries and trades. We have much to be
> grateful for and much to offer the world at large.
>
> Within this American society is a fast-paced culture that
> claims the *here and now*, sometimes with a vengeance. We
> go from point A to point B often without forethought or
> reflection. We chase the American dream with clearly-
> defined goals, visionary mission statements, and ambitious
> climbs of the ladder.
>
> We love noise. I've always joked about being pop-
> culturally challenged, but I had never realized my hand-
> icap as fully as I did when I arrived at the Miami airport
> on July 3rd. After eight weeks away from the noise, I did
> not have a clue. I felt overwhelmed by the barrage of cell
> phones, laptops, televisions, and other electronic devices.
> We really do love noise. We wake up to the radio, brush
> our teeth to *Good Morning America*, watch the news on

the internet, and even fall asleep watching reruns of our
favorite TV shows.

But how often do our ears hear the softening whispers
of silence? How often do we embrace the sweet songs of
solitude? Do we take time to be still and experience peace
in its fullness? I came across the following Mother Teresa
quote several months ago, but it has never had more
meaning than it does now: "The fruit of silence is prayer.
The fruit of prayer is faith. The fruit of faith is love. The
fruit of love is service. The fruit of service is peace."[8]

As you can imagine, my transition back into American life has been quick in some ways and slow in others.
I am still adjusting. For those whom I have yet to talk
to, I am healthy, happy, and busy with camp and travels.
Tomorrow evening, I leave for Italy with my family for
two weeks. We're circling the Italian boot, beginning and
ending in Rome. As it is our first time in Europe as a family, it should be a vacation to remember.

In the midst of it all, I realize that the logic of love is
counterintuitive, countercultural, and certainly counter-
American. To steal Mother Teresa's words again, the
more we have, the less we give. And the less we have,
the more we give. I saw this truth in the people of Honduras, and I see it in myself as an American. In our simplicity there is abundance. In our self-denial there is true
love. In our simplicity there is life.

As I learned that summer, leisure frees us up to no longer
be afraid of service, sacrifice, or suffering because we know
they are the surest precursors to joy. Time, wisdom, and
experience have taught us so. In fact, leisure at its heights
reminds us that God took on human flesh and poured out
every last drop of his blood on a Cross. What could be
more absurd? Josef Pieper explains, "In leisure, there is,

---

[8] Mother Teresa, *A Simple Path* (New York: Ballantine Books, 1995), p. 1.

furthermore, something of the serenity of 'not-being-able-to-grasp,' of the recognition of the mysterious character of the world, and the confidence of blind faith, which can let things go as they will."[9] Against all human logic, Christ's death led to our salvation. Now, our faith in him pierces the veil behind which we see his glory everywhere.

Leisure in its truest form is the worship of Almighty God that not only fixes our eyes on the horizon but brings heaven to Earth. It's the power to step beyond the world around us and come into contact with divine love as the foundation of all reality. Leisure keeps our religious sense alive and provides the foundation of all authentic culture. After all, the root word of culture is *cult* (which literally means "worship"). Given this fact, the vital importance of beautiful churches and sacred liturgies dedicated to the worship of God cannot be exaggerated.

Ultimately, leisure allows us to let go and trust that God is the protagonist of our lives. It's an invitation to stillness and intentionality. It affects how we work, when we rest, what music we enjoy, which movies we watch, and how we worship. It doesn't mean we suddenly listen to nothing but chant music and exclusively read the lives of the saints. Rather, it's an invitation to live with a sacramental imagination, to fix our eyes constantly on the horizon and find the glory of God even in the most ordinary of circumstances.

Leisure is a wonderful culmination point for our first five principles. Not only does leisure cultivate *wonder*, but wonder cultivates leisure. They work hand-in-hand. Leisure also provides a testing ground for interior *freedom*. How easily and joyfully do we choose virtue in moments of profound stillness and leisure? Where do our hearts'

---

[9] Pieper, *Leisure*, p. 31.

affections land when the busyness dies down? Additionally, when leisure is shared by virtuous *friends*, it transforms into festivity. Live music, great feasts, and shared adventures are all beautiful examples of festivity, where friends intentionally enter into leisure together. Finally, leisure is a prerequisite for contemplative *prayer* and the source of festivity in heaven, where we'll join all the saints and angels in the eternal worship of God. As we move into the next principle of *work*, it will become increasingly obvious how these first five principles are beautifully interwoven and lay the foundation for the rest to come.

ALL SHALL BE WELL

It's been many years since my first Cuban cigar, and I'll never forget how it led me to a place of contemplation that night in Antigua with a great friend by my side. To this day, I revel in all the profound truths I learned about leisure that summer while serving the poorest and happiest people I've ever known. Given how busy and fast-paced my life has been ever since, I need to relearn these truths. I need to relearn how to take Sunday afternoon naps in hammocks and build true leisure into my daily rhythm. All of us are made to appreciate a rose in bloom, enjoy live music with friends, and master the art of storytelling around a bonfire. We need leisure to awaken our senses so our culture of noise doesn't distract or enslave us.

While faith is necessary to worship God, all the lower forms of leisure involving music, creativity, food, and study are as accessible to nonbelievers as our first three principles of wonder, freedom, and friendship. You don't have to be a Christian to see the beauty of a well-cultivated imagination, heroic virtue, authentic relationship, and intentional leisure. They all lead to truth and goodness and eventually to Jesus Christ himself. Therefore, they are important means to cultivating the art of being human and powerful entry points for evangelizing our post-Christian world.

In the final analysis, true leisure points us to God, who rested on the seventh day and delighted in his creation. We must do the same. In a world obsessed with work, technology, money, and science, we need apostles of the interior life who remind others to rejoice in their existence, not their productivity. We must reject sloth on one end and all tendencies toward busyness on the other. Leisure alone protects us from the dangerous vice of acedia and fosters our receptivity to the true, the good, and the beautiful. It places our soul at rest so that we can look out at the world as easily as we look into our souls and say with humble confidence, "All shall be well, and all shall be well, and all manner of things shall be well."[10]

GETTING PRACTICAL

- Curate your music, books, movies, and art based on a standard of leisure, not entertainment. Make sure they reflect and transcend reality, inspiring you toward virtue and joy.
- Cut down on hobbies that are at best a waste of your time and replace them with hobbies that dispose you to truth, beauty, and goodness.
- Develop the habit of intellectual leisure. Read through our recommended books for fifteen minutes a day. Start a book club. Get your friends together once a month to discuss big philosophical ideas.

[10] Julian of Norwich, *Revelations of Divine Love* (London: Ballantyne Press, 1902), p. 51.

- Learn a musical instrument. You don't have to be great at it. Simply delight in the act of co-creating with God.
- Find a beautiful park near you and disappear for a long weekend of hiking and camping with family or friends.
- Find the most beautiful church in your area and worship there next Sunday, or spend an hour there in quiet prayer at some point this week.

FURTHER READING

Guardini, Romano. *Letters from Lake Como: Explorations in Technology and the Human Race.* Translated by Geoffrey W. Bromiley. Grand Rapids, MI: W. B. Eerdmans, 1994.

Nault, Dom Jean-Charles, O.S.B. *The Noonday Devil: Acedia, the Unnamed Evil of Our Times.* Translated by Michael J. Miller. San Francisco: Ignatius Press, 2015.

Pieper, Josef. *Leisure: The Basis of Culture.* South Bend, IN: St. Augustine's Press, 1998.

Schall, James V. *On the Unseriousness of Human Affairs: Teaching, Writing, Playing, Believing, Lecturing, Philosophizing, Singing, Dancing.* Wilmington, DE: Intercollegiate Studies Institute, 2012.

Chapter 6

Work

wɔrk | *noun* | *activity involving mental or physical effort done in order to achieve a purpose or result.*

Only once have I traveled round-trip to Europe and back in fewer than seventy-two hours. Like any sane person, I prefer to maximize my time in other parts of the world and dive into their cultures as much as possible. It was September 2010, and I was recovering from a breakup. I was looking for an escape. Within two weeks of that relationship ending, one of my best friends from England invited me across the pond to join him for the beatification of John Henry Newman. I didn't hesitate. I asked for a few days off work, bought a last-minute flight, and began reading every Newman sermon I could get my hands on in preparation for the trip.

Now canonized, Saint John Henry Newman is the most famous Anglican convert to the Catholic faith of the nineteenth century. Because of my own deepening conversion that took place while studying abroad in England, he has always been a hero and a role model. I first heard about him at the Brompton Oratory on the southwest side of London. Because I went there frequently for daily Mass while studying abroad, I slowly came to know the Oratorians and their most famous English convert, whose legacy is enshrined in the form of a statue by the entrance of this Romanesque church. Over time, I devoured many of Newman's writings, such as *Apologia Pro Vita Sua* and *Parochial and Plain Sermons*. Having the opportunity to go to his beatification—all the while enjoying the first-ever state visit by a pope to Britain—was a total dream.

The night before the beatification, Pope Benedict XVI gathered with thousands of young people in Hyde Park for Eucharistic Adoration. In a brief exhortation, Benedict XVI held up Newman's life as a profound reminder "that if we have accepted the truth of Christ and committed our lives to him, there can be no separation between what we believe and the way we live our lives."[1] He went on to share one of Newman's most famous meditations on the dignity of work, highlighting the unique and unrepeatable calling of every human person to offer "some definite service" to God with his life. The Holy Father continued:

> No one who looks realistically at our world today could think that Christians can afford to go on with business as usual, ignoring the profound crisis of faith which has overtaken our society, or simply trusting that the patrimony of values handed down by the Christian centuries will continue to inspire and shape the future of our society. We know that in times of crisis and upheaval God has raised up great saints and prophets for the renewal of the Church and Christian society; we trust in his providence and we pray for his continued guidance. But each of us, in accordance with his or her state of life, is called to work for the

[1] Benedict XVI, Apostolic Journey to the United Kingdom: Prayer Vigil on the Eve of the Beatification of Cardinal John Henry Newman (address, Hyde Park, London, September 18, 2010), https://www.vatican.va/content /benedict-xvi/en/speeches/2010/september/documents/hf_ben-xvi_spe _20100918_veglia-card-newman.html.

advancement of God's Kingdom by imbuing temporal life
with the values of the Gospel. Each of us has a mission,
each of us is called to change the world, to work for a
culture of life, a culture forged by love and respect for the
dignity of each human person.[2]

If not for these words convicting me and lifting my
spirit at such a critical juncture in life, there is no telling
where I would be today. At that point, I was one year
out of seminary, a few weeks out of a serious relationship,
and uncertain about most areas of my life. By the grace of
God, I never stopped praying. I was open to his will in a
desperate way. In fact, there was one aspect of my life that
still had total clarity and joy: mentoring young people in
virtue and helping them fall in love with God. I decided
that day to double down on this work. If it wasn't time
for me to know my vocation yet, I could at least confi-
dently focus my energy on forming the next generation
after God's own heart. This work took on many different
forms and carried me through the next decade of my life,
never ceasing to bring great joy and bear much fruit. Even
now, it remains the greatest privilege of my life.

ORIGINAL GLORY

We are all made for work. Work is an inherent part of
being human after the Fall. It's part of our dignity as sons
and daughters created in the image of God, and it looks
different for everyone. We all have talents, limitations,
and life experiences that coalesce into a unique offering
to be brought into the world. Whether working every

---

[2] Ibid.

day at a desk, in a field, or on the internet, work gives us dignity and purpose. It connects us back to our original glory, before sin came into the picture and turned life into labor.

At the beginning of creation, God said, "Let us make man in our image, after our likeness; and let them have dominion over the fish of the sea, and over the birds of the air, and over the cattle, and over all the earth" (Gen 1:26). Whether we are students, baristas, lawyers, or stay-at-home moms, all of us are called to reflect the creativity of God in our work. We all have a part to play in declaring dominion over creation and ordering the world toward God's greater glory. Dominion is not domination but stewardship, transforming what God has entrusted to us into a sacrifice of praise. This truth is built into every part-time job and lifelong career path. It's the very reason that work can always be joyful and fulfilling.

Only because of the Fall of mankind has life become laborious. Only because of sin do we associate work with the idea of occupation rather than vocation. It's not meant merely to occupy time or pay the bills. Human work is a participation in divine work. It's a calling from God that gives us dignity and enables us to contribute to the good of society. According to Saint John Paul II in his encyclical *Laborem Exercens*, work transforms nature and makes us more human:

> [Work] is not only good in the sense that it is useful or something to enjoy; it is also good as being something worthy, that is to say, something that corresponds to man's dignity, that expresses this dignity and increases it. If one wishes to define more clearly the ethical meaning of work, it is this truth that one must particularly keep in mind. Work is a good thing for man—a good thing for his humanity—because through work man *not only transforms*

nature, adapting it to his own needs, but he also *achieves fulfilment* as a human being and indeed, in a sense, becomes "more a human being."[3]

We often hold up work as a necessary evil when it's in fact an objective good. As the pope explains, it brings fulfillment to the human soul and glory to our heavenly Father. On the flip side, work can easily become an idol. If we fail to integrate it with leisure, work can become our sole identity and overtake our primary vocation. It can become a source of vanity and greed rather than an opportunity for personal growth and service to others.

It's important to remember that work is connected to our vocation but not synonymous with it. It's secondary to our primary vocation as a spouse, parent, priest, or religious. For example, as much as a married man might enjoy being a missionary and fundraising his salary, he should never do so to the detriment of his wife and children. Work is the means by which he provides for his family, and their souls are always his primary responsibility. On the other hand, work can never be reduced to mere function. Work is always more than a wage. As long as the Lord is involved, it is always and everywhere a calling. — Casey's new do

The sheer variety of work in the world says everything about God's creativity. You can till the soil while another produces legal documents. You can raise children while another writes political speeches. If you're a full-time student right now, *that's* your work. Regardless, "whatever you do, in word or deed, do everything in the name of the Lord Jesus, giving thanks to God the Father through him" (Col 3:17). What you do matters less than the spirit with

[3] John Paul II, Encyclical on Human Work *Laborem Exercens* (September 14, 1981), no. 9 (emphasis in original), https://www.vatican.va/content/john-paul-ii/en/encyclicals/documents/hf_jp-ii_enc_14091981_laborem-exercens.html.

expectation

which you do it. There is an objective dimension to work, and it's important to rejoice in whatever is accomplished through the work of your hands. However, the subjective dimension is far more important, as work enables you to fulfill your humanity and exercise your gifts for the greater glory of God.[4]

Additionally, work reminds us that we're not alone in the world. We're not self-sustaining. We depend on God, others, and institutions to find fulfillment in life. Our next principle of *community* is similarly built on this truth. In an opinion piece for the *New York Times* several years ago, Ross Douthat drew a connection between the sharp rise of suicide among middle-aged men and their lack of belonging to larger organizations:

> As the University of Virginia sociologist Brad Wilcox pointed out recently, there's a strong link between suicide and weakened social ties: people—and especially men— become more likely to kill themselves "when they get disconnected from society's core institutions (e.g., marriage, religion) or when their economic prospects take a dive (e.g., unemployment)." That's exactly what we've seen happen lately among the middle-aged male population, whose suicide rates have climbed the fastest: a retreat from family obligations, from civic and religious participation, and from full-time paying work.[5]

Without work, man drifts through his day-to-day life without much purpose. Before long, he drifts away from the very people and institutions he depends on for happiness. For those who are blessed with hard work, even the most challenging days are a path to glory. The most

---

[4] Ibid., no. 6.

[5] Ross Douthat, "All the Lonely People", *New York Times*, May 18, 2013, https://www.nytimes.com/2013/05/19/opinion/sunday/douthat-loneliness-and-suicide.html.

thankless of tasks are an opportunity to depend on others and rejoice in our dignity as co-creators with God.

[handwritten note: I haven't talked that opportunities much.]

WORK AS SANCTIFICATION

I'll never forget the first time I heard that ordinary work could lead to extraordinary grace. I was back on my college campus after months of studying abroad, bored with my studies and looking for every adventure I could find. After spending more time out of the country than in it, I was restless when anything seemed routine or commonplace. Then one day our university chaplain invited me to participate in a day-long retreat led by a member of Opus Dei. At that point, my only understanding of Opus Dei came from Dan Brown's infamous novel *The Da Vinci Code*, which was a thrill to read but deceptive in its portrayal of the personal prelature founded by Saint Josemaría Escrivá in 1928. Intrigued by the potential for controversy, I gladly committed to the retreat.

That day, there were fewer than ten of us gathered, all university students apart from one high school student. Fourteen years later, I came across my notes from this retreat and realized how profoundly it shaped my life from that point forward. Before encountering Opus Dei, I had instincts about the Church's universal call to holiness and our daily opportunity to become great saints amid our ordinary circumstances. My identity was already founded on beloved sonship, what Opus Dei termed *divine filiation*. I was living the apostolate of friendship and knew how powerfully God could communicate his love to others through it. While on retreat that day, I learned that all these ideas were fundamental to Opus Dei—universal holiness, beloved sonship, and evangelization through friendship. But I had never, not once in my entire life, heard their founder's teachings on the *sanctification of work*.

According to it, all work is an extension of *prayer* (our fourth principle) and a means of giving glory to God. For a student, the desk is his altar of sacrifice. For the farmer, it's his plow. For the lawyer, it's his persuasive arguments. Work can also be a powerful form of intercessory prayer as one lifts up particular tasks or periods of work for the needs and intentions of others. Daily work also sanctifies us with its countless opportunities for growth in fortitude, prudence, charity, hope, justice, and other virtues (cultivating our second principle of *freedom*). Hearing all these ideas while on retreat years ago was revolutionary to me.

In a homily given at the University of Navarra in 1967, Saint Josemaría quotes Saint Paul, reminding everyone present to "do all to the glory of God" (1 Cor 10:31). He then goes on to explain:

This doctrine of Holy Scripture, as you know, is to be found in the very nucleus of the spirit of Opus Dei. It leads you to do your work as perfectly as possible, to love God and mankind by putting love in the little things of everyday life, and discovering that divine something which is hidden in small details. The lines of a Castilian poet are especially appropriate here: "Write slowly and with a careful hand, for doing things well is more important than doing them" (Machado, A., *Poesías Completas, CLXI—Proverbios y cantares, XXIV*, Espasa Calpe, Madrid, 1940).

I assure you, my sons and daughters, that when a Christian carries out with love the most insignificant everyday action, that action overflows with the transcendence of God. That is why I have told you repeatedly, and hammered away once and again on the idea that the Christian vocation consists of making heroic verse out of the prose of each day. Heaven and earth seem to merge, my sons and daughters, on the horizon. But where they really meet is in your hearts, when you sanctify your everyday lives.[6]

Our commitment to virtue and excellence should carry over into every aspect of our academic and professional lives. Whether toiling in an office, workshop, or studio, we all have a daily altar of sacrifice that is meant to sanctify us. Our attention to detail, our perseverance through difficult tasks, and our willingness to be hidden as we labor are all powerful means of sanctification.

While it's tempting to think that tougher work leads to greater sanctity, it's important to remember that with virtue comes ease and spontaneity—even in our work. If we're growing in virtue, then our toughest work will get easier over time and bring even more grace to the soul. Ultimately, work sanctifies us not because it's difficult but because it's good. It's part of God's original plan for all of us.

I would be remiss to not bring up Saint Joseph in the context of this sixth principle. He's not only the foster father of our Lord Jesus Christ but also the great patron of workers. Think of all the years he spent with Jesus in the carpentry shop. Like Saint Joseph, we can be recollected at every moment of our workday as long as we keep Jesus by our side.

FROM MAGNANIMITY TO MISSION

Every great work, from the building of St. Peter's Basilica to the founding of America, requires greatness of

---

[6]Josemaría Escrivá, "Homily: Passionately Loving the World", Opus Dei (website), https://opusdei.org/en-us/article/passionately-loving-the-world-2/.

+ hitting a single

soul—what's known as the virtue of magnanimity. It's rare in our culture of comfort, but it's at the heart of every saint who has ever done something remarkable for the Lord. From the growth of religious communities to the feeding of the poor, there has never been a great saint without magnanimity. In his book *Created for Greatness*, leadership expert Alexandre Havard describes it as follows:

> Magnanimity is the conquest of greatness. It is not content to initiate; it achieves. It is not content to aspire to greatness, but to attain it. It is like jet fuel: it is the propulsive virtue *par excellence*. Magnanimity is the virtue of action; there is more energy in it than in mere audacity. The magnanimous person achieves self-fulfillment in and through action. He gives himself over to it with passion and enthusiasm.
>
> For the true leader, action always stems from self-awareness. It is never mere *activism*, and never degenerates into *workaholism*. Leaders are always *doers*, but never do things just for the sake of doing them; their doing is always an extension of their being, the outgrowth of their contemplation of their own dignity and greatness.[7]

Our work is always an overflow of our identity, not the other way around. Being precedes doing, just as greatness of soul precedes greatness of work. At every season of our lives, God invites us to echo the words of the Blessed Mother during her visitation to Elizabeth, "For he who is mighty has done great things for me, and holy is his name" (Lk 1:49). If our lives are rooted in prayer and punctuated with leisure, we'll never have any confusion about Who is doing all the great work in us and through us. It is God

[7] Alexandre Havard, *Created for Greatness: The Power of Magnanimity* (New Rochelle, NY: Scepter, 2014), pp. 13–14 (emphasis in original).

who does great things. *He* is the One who makes it all happen. Our part is simply to acknowledge our nothingness before his greatness and say yes every day to his beautiful plan for our lives.

In his classic book *Humility of Heart*, Father Cajetan Mary da Bergamo compares the prideful man to a thief. As soon as he dares to claim God's glory as his own, the prideful man is living a delusion. Father Cajetan writes, "If I am proud, I become like a thief, appropriating to myself that which is not mine but God's. And most assuredly it is a greater sin to rob God of that which belongs to God than to rob man of that which is man's."[8] All our work—even when it involves our own sweat, toil, and tears—is a cooperation with God's grace. If we do not have humility mingled with magnanimity, God will not bless our noblest of desires nor our greatest endeavors. For any work to bear great fruit, it must be constantly purified by the Lord and executed for his glory alone.

When others see us living this principle of work, it becomes a powerful way to spread the Gospel. They'll see our joy and attention to detail when we tackle the most challenging of tasks. It'll remind them of the beauty and creativity with which God created the heavens and the earth. They'll see our desire for greatness, our willingness to sacrifice, and our humble surrendering to God the Father. It'll remind them of the Lord Jesus Christ, whose greatest work was the sacrifice of his life for the salvation of the world.

Our world is plagued by activism and sloth, which are two sides of the same vicious coin of acedia. To live

---

[8] Cajetan Mary da Bergamo, *Humility of Heart*, trans. Hebert Cardinal Vaughn, ed. Paul A. Boer (Edmond, OK: Veritatis Splendor Publications, 2012), p. 20.

beautiful lives that evangelize our culture of noise, we must integrate leisure and work into our daily lives. Through leisure, we remember that we're more than just our accomplishments. Through work, we cultivate the virtue of magnanimity even as we remember our total dependency on God. It's in this way that work makes every moment holy. It gives us an opportunity to unite our sacrifice of praise with that of the Lord Jesus Christ. It brings us out of ourselves and inspires us to fight for the original glory we once enjoyed in the Garden of Eden. And when we bring others into this fight, we begin living our next principle of *community* without even realizing it.

With that in mind, it seems only appropriate to leave the last word to Saint John Henry Newman, whose meditation on work inspired thousands gathered in Hyde Park eleven years ago and countless others since its first publication in 1848:

God has created me to do Him some definite service; He has committed some work to me which He has not committed to another. I have my mission—I never may know it in this life, but I shall be told it in the next. Somehow I am necessary for His purposes, as necessary in my place as an Archangel in his—if, indeed, I fail, He can raise another, as He could make the stones children of Abraham. Yet I have a part in this great work; I am a link in a chain, a bond of connexion between persons. He has not created me for naught. I shall do good, I shall do His work; I shall be an angel of peace, a preacher of truth in my own place, while not intending it, if I do but keep His commandments and serve Him in my calling.

Therefore I will trust Him. Whatever, wherever I am, I can never be thrown away. If I am in sickness, my sickness may serve Him; in perplexity, my perplexity may serve Him; if I am in sorrow, my sorrow may serve Him. My sickness, or perplexity, or sorrow may be necessary causes of some great end, which is quite beyond us. He does nothing in vain; He may prolong my life, He may shorten it; He knows what He is about. He may take away my friends, He may throw me among strangers, He may make me feel desolate, make my spirits sink, hide the future from me—still He knows what He is about.[9]

Indeed. The Lord knows what he's about and has created each of us to do him some definite work for his greater glory. May the truth of his providence and perfect plan for our lives rest deep in our hearts.

GETTING PRACTICAL

- Saint Ignatius of Loyola is often quoted as saying, "Pray as if everything depended on God and work as if everything depended on you."[10] How does that maxim play itself out in your life?
- Take great pride in your attention to detail. It's in the ordinary pursuit of excellence that God is glorified.
- Become more aware of God's presence while you're at work. Much like Saint Joseph, you can turn every task into a prayer as long as you keep the Lord Jesus with you.
- Every day, subordinate your work to your primary vocation. Never let it overtake your responsibility to lead the souls entrusted to you to heaven.

[9] John Henry Newman, "Part III, Meditations on Christian Doctrine with a Visit to the Blessed Sacrament before Meditation", March 7, 1848, in *Newman Reader—Works of John Henry Newman*, National Institute for Newman Studies, 2007, https://www.newmanreader.org/works/meditations/meditations9.html.

[10] Attributed to Saint Ignatius Loyola, in Joseph de Guibert, S.J., *The Jesuits: Their Spiritual Doctrine and Practice* (Chicago: Loyola University Press, 1964), 148n55.

- Regularly surrender your current or future career to God and ask what he wants for you. Always look for work that utilizes your gifts but acknowledges your limitations.

FURTHER READING

Hahn, Scott. *Ordinary Work, Extraordinary Grace: My Spiritual Journey in Opus Dei*. New York: Doubleday, 2006.

Havard, Alexandre. *Created for Greatness: The Power of Magnanimity*. New Rochelle, NY: Scepter, 2014.

John Paul II. Encyclical on Human Work *Laborem Exercens*. September 14, 1981. https://www.vatican.va/content/john-paul-ii/en/encyclicals/documents/hf_jp-ii_enc_14091981_laborem-exercens.html.

Naughton, Michael J. *Getting Work Right: Labor and Leisure in a Fragmented World*. Steubenville, OH: Emmaus Road Publishing, 2019.

Pearce, Joseph. *Small Is Still Beautiful: Economics as if Families Mattered*. Wilmington, DE: ISI Books, 2006.

Chapter 7

Community

kə'myoonədē | noun | a feeling of fellowship with others, as a result of sharing common attitudes, interests, and goals.

"You have two options," I said to the young man. "You either wiggle your way out of this crack or you stay in this cave forever." A small group of us were spelunking near a Carthusian monastery outside of Vienna, Austria. It was the last day of a three-week pilgrimage, and one of our young confrères was stuck in the final crack that separated the largest cavern from the cave's entrance. We had all made it through the crack on our way into the cave, but now gravity was working against us as we climbed our way out. We were on the brink of exhaustion and almost late for a bus ride to a swimming hole with a hundred other young men on pilgrimage.

I was the assumed leader of the group and found myself fighting every temptation to panic. The blood was rushing to my head as I turned my body around, lodged my feet against the wall for leverage, and began pulling this young man through the crack. The guys behind him were pushing with all their might. Nobody appeared nervous, but I was increasingly aware of the magnitude of the situation. We had to get this young man out, and he was at the end of his strength. I began harnessing the power of the entire group as I yelled for them to push harder. We were at a standstill. Nothing seemed to be enough to bring this young man out of the crack and into freedom. Meanwhile, his friends behind him were lost in their delight of being thousands of miles away from home, chanting prayers and singing songs with genuine jubilation. They were totally oblivious to the seriousness of the situation, even as they pushed with every fiber of their being.

Though it felt like an eternity, we spent several more minutes strategizing and collaborating before this young man was finally set free. The rest of the guys made their way through the crack with considerable effort but far greater ease. We were covered in mud as we approached the mouth of the cave and began running through the Austrian hills so as to not be late for the bus. When we showed up just on time but filthy from head to toe, the bus driver insisted that we rinse off in a nearby creek. We already knew the creek's water was frigid, as many of us had jumped into it the day before. We smiled at each other with exasperation, quickly washed off in the creek, and boarded the bus only to fall asleep in the last row with a half-eaten tub of peanut butter in our hands. Our nerves were shot, but our hearts were full.

We became a band of brothers that day. Though we hadn't known each other well before the pilgrimage, our shared experience in the cave solidified our sense of community for life. Because of what we overcame together, we were now connected to each other. We shared a memory so singular and unique that it bonded us for life. More importantly, that memory was made possible only by our shared association with a larger institution—namely, the Catholic high school that led the pilgrimage. Because the sense of community ran so deep by the end of the trip, several of us have never lost touch.

UNDERSTANDING HUMAN NATURE

Though we live in an individualistic age, we throw around the word *community* all the time in reference to work, school, neighborhood, and friends. There's something deep in every human heart, even among the most introverted of personalities, that longs for connection to a place and a community. Even if we enjoy the greatest of friendships, we need more than individual friends for human happiness and flourishing. We need a band of brothers and sisters, an interconnected community of family and friends. The desire to belong is built into our human nature. Because we are made in the image and likeness of God, who is a communion of Persons, it makes sense that we will never thrive without intentional community.

It's easy to romanticize about what community might have been like at other times in history. My mind immediately goes to 1960s Mayberry, the idyllic hometown of *The Andy Griffith Show*, where every day culminated on a front porch with sweet tea. America sixty years ago had its fair share of problems, just as America today enjoys its fair share of blessings, but the time we're living through now is undoubtedly a time of greater isolation. People often have more of a connection with their screens than they do with their families. Many don't know the names of their neighbors or the people who sit next to them in the pews on Sunday. More and more people work remotely. Loneliness is on the rise.

Even Hitler understood the devastating effects of isolation and seized it as an opportunity for manipulation. In his autobiographical manifesto *Mein Kampf*, he wrote, "The mass meeting is necessary if only for the reason that in it the individual, who in becoming an adherent of a new movement feels lonely and is easily seized with the fear of being alone, receives for the first time the picture of a greater community, something that has a strengthening and an encouraging effect on most people."[1] It's a basic truth of our human nature. Life apart from membership in a larger community can feel intolerable. For good or for ill, there will always be organizations and institutions that rise up to meet the need we all have for belonging.

Our culture of isolation is not entirely the fault of social media, which has often fooled us into thinking that online communities are real communities. It's not even the fault of political parties, which often usurp power from local communities to build bureaucracies that promise security and prosperity. Nor is it the lack of good schools, neighborhood associations, and local coffee shops. All those secondary institutions are important, and while many of them are in need of profound renewal, the two institutions most responsible for the lack of deep and meaningful community in our world today are the family and the Church. In his 2019 book *Getting Work Right*, Michael Naughton describes them as the primary institutions of society:

> Family founded in marriage is the first vital cell of society in which economic and political institutions should be embedded. John Paul II tells us that the family is the place where we receive the first formative ideas about "what it means to love and to be loved, and thus what it actually means to be a person" (John Paul II, Encyclical Letter on the Hundredth Anniversary of *Rerum novarum*

[1] Adolf Hitler, *Mein Kampf*, cited in Franz L. Neumann, *Behemoth: The Structure and Practice of National Socialism 1933–1954* (New York: Octagon Books, 1972), p. 358.

Centesimus annus [May 1, 1991], ¶ 38). The family should be the place where we first experience goods shared in common.

Yet, the family needs something more than itself. The family by itself is prone to its parochialism and tribalism and can insulate itself from the larger good of society. Like any ecosystem, institutions are dependent on other systems. Institutions need help from other institutions to flourish. When isolated, they tend to implode. The family, in particular, needs a transcendent source to connect it to the common good and to help it resist the tendency to self-absorption. That source is expressed through the institution of religion—in particular, the Church.[2]

If the family and the Church don't live up to their roles as primary institutions, they leave behind a massive vacuum filled by social entrepreneurs, political ideologues, and idealistic technocrats. That describes our post-Christian culture today. If we're not careful, the void of loneliness will eventually be filled by the state. In the words of Robert Nisbet in *The Quest for Community*, "The extraordinary accomplishments of totalitarianism in the twentieth century would be inexplicable were it not for the immense, burning appeal it exerts upon masses of individuals who have lost, or had taken away, their accustomed roots of membership and belief."[3] We shouldn't be surprised by the soft totalitarianism of our age. Countless citizens acquiesce as governments assert more and more control over their day-to-day lives. Even in America, some hardly blink an eye at statewide mandates

[2] Michael J. Naughton, *Getting Work Right: Labor and Leisure in a Fragmented World* (Steubenville, OH: Emmaus Road Publishing, 2019), pp. 59–60.

[3] Robert A. Nisbet, *The Quest for Community: A Study in the Ethics of Order and Freedom* (Wilmington, DE: ISI Books, 1953), p. 186.

or executive orders anymore. What does the future of democracy look like in a citizenry so dependent on the state for its moral guidance and sense of belonging? Are we any less vulnerable to manipulation than the people of Germany just under a century ago? Regardless of the answer, we're at a cultural and political crossroads. We need a massive renewal of family life and faith for our democracy to survive.

NO MAN IS AN ISLAND

Community became a nonnegotiable part of life during my summer of missionary work halfway through my college years. For the first time ever, I was living, praying, and working in community with five other young adults who were responsible for coordinating the work of hundreds of teenagers as they came down on their short-term mission trips. The days were long but deeply rewarding. The five of us depended on each other for meals, work projects, and day-to-day support. There was no way we could be faithful to our mission in Honduras without our community providing strength for us and inspiration for others. While I had a sense of belonging back home in Atlanta, where I grew up, and in Nashville, where I went to college, that missionary community was unlike anything I had ever experienced. It was rooted in *prayer* (our fourth principle) and oriented toward *mission* (our ninth principle). It was fulfilling and exhilarating in ways I never thought possible.

At the end of that summer, I left to study abroad and quickly found myself reflecting on the essential role of community in my life. Halfway through that semester, I

wrote a blog about the idea of home and the importance
of belonging to others. Below is an excerpt:

As I feel more and more settled in London, the idea of
home takes on new depth and breathes life into my existence as a foreigner living abroad. Though thousands of
miles from Atlanta and Nashville and surrounded by seven
million strangers a day, I still feel the peace that comes
through fellowship and love amid family and friends. I do
not understand this peace, nor can I can explain it away.
But it is very real. John Henry Newman often considered himself least lonely when he was most alone. His
eyes were always set on the horizon of the unseen, where
loneliness fades and mysticism takes root. It is *this* mindset that allows for peace, that (in the words of St. John
Vianney) allows miles to melt before the tabernacle.

At the moment, I am sitting inside a café at the Pontifical Gregorian University in Roma, Italia. I am surrounded
by the rhythmic pulse of black, white, and brown clerics—
belonging to seminarians, priests, monks, and brothers—as
they frequent the café in 45-minute waves between classes.
Occasionally a nun in her habit walks by and leaves me
stunned. After arriving in the Eternal City around 1:00 PM
yesterday, a dear friend picked me up and took me to his
apartment within spitting distance of the Vatican Museum.
After a quick lunch, we walked the ancient pilgrim path
from St. Peter's Square to the Coliseum to the Janiculum,
where we met up with several seminarians at the North
American College for Vespers and dinner. Needless to say,
I feel like a five-year-old in a candy store.

That being said, most of the past month was spent in
exploration of England, bringing me to the calm splendor
of Canterbury Cathedral and the wild beauty of gorge-
scrambling in Keswick. My love for the city of London
grows every day. Having now been visited by my dad

three weeks ago and a good friend from Atlanta this past weekend, I feel like I have finally shared a piece of London with home. Similarly, visiting friends in Scotland was a taste of homecoming, and the anticipation of my entire family coming at Thanksgiving only grows by the week!

At the end of the day, my grateful heart beats steadily in paradox. I am learning how to embrace wisdom and folly—to live *in* the here and now but *for* the mystical horizon. I am learning how to embrace the intellect *and* the spirit—to be challenged by views different from my own *and* rest in my own convictions. In the end, I always want to desire the peaceful simplicity of a child and the fierce strength of a warrior—a paradox indeed!

Though written fifteen years ago, those words articulate my deepest insights into community today. No man is an island. We cannot *do life* alone. It's no coincidence that I stumbled into these realizations during the same season of life that I began attending daily Mass. It didn't matter the country, language, or culture. As long as I could find the Eucharist, I was at home. Those European basilicas were not only breathtaking but also a remedy for my loneliness. The habit of daily Mass that developed during that semester abroad has sustained me ever since, providing my most significant sense of belonging wherever I am. There is nothing more unifying than the common worship of fellow Christians who unite their hearts every day with the Eucharistic Lord.

We all long for a sense of home, belonging, and community. The difficulty is finding parishes, schools, workplaces, and neighborhoods that provide it. Sin divides the human heart; so too it divides the hearts of many institutions. How do we know if a place is built on healthy community? How can we go about building healthy community where it doesn't currently exist?

KEY MARKS OF HEALTHY COMMUNITY

Depending on their leadership and culture, communities can be hotbeds for scandal or strongholds for conversion. When the latter is the case, they preserve and expand Christian culture. Think about the greatest religious communities of the last fifteen hundred years. From the Benedictines to the Carthusians, they all mastered community life during their peaks and left behind legacies of holiness that the world will never stop contemplating. Thanks be to God, the father of Western monasticism wrote down his community's way of life in what later became known as *The Rule of St. Benedict*. In this rule, one can find all the key marks of healthy community, as applicable to families, businesses, and other organizations as they are to monasteries.

Before we dive into the rule, let's consider these harrowing words delivered by Robert Cardinal Sarah in Paris only six weeks after the tragic burning of Notre-Dame Cathedral in 2019:

> I am convinced that this civilization is living through its mortal hour. As once during the decline and fall of Rome, so today the elites care for nothing but increasing the luxury of their daily lives, and the people have been anesthetized by every more vulgar entertainments....
>
> Behold modern man: alone, wandering about in a field of ruins....
>
> We must find places where the virtues can flourish. It is time to rediscover the courage of non-conformism. Christians must create places where the air is breathable, or simply where the Christian life is possible. I call upon Christians to bravely open oases of freedom in the midst of the desert created by rampant profiteering. Indeed you must not be alone in the desert of a society without God. A Christian who stays alone is a Christian in

122 LET BEAUTY SPEAK

danger! He will end up being devoured by the sharks of the market society. Christians must regroup in communities around their cathedrals: the houses of God. Our communities must put God in the center. At the center of our lives, our thoughts, our actions, our liturgies, and our cathedrals.[4]

Indeed, our faith has no chance of survival without communities centered on God. Cardinal Sarah is reminding us of the same truth that Saint Benedict wrote about fifteen centuries ago. In the opening chapters of his *Rule*, he commands all the monks to "treasure chastity, harbor neither hatred nor jealousy of anyone, and do nothing out of envy".[5] He continues, "Do not love quarreling; shun arrogance. Respect the elders and love the young. Pray for your enemies out of love for Christ. If you have a dispute with someone, make peace with him before the sun goes down."[6] He goes on to dedicate entire sections to obedience, restraint of speech, care for the sick, reception of guests, and daily allowance for food and wine. Imagine if every home, business, and parish strove to build their communities based on these rules. Imagine the peace we would enjoy if the Beatitudes (Mt 5:1–12) were the basis for all our attitudes and behaviors. Imagine the sheer

[4] Robert Cardinal Sarah, cited in "Cardinal Sarah: 'We Must Rebuild the Cathedral.... We Do Not Need to Invent a New Church'", trans. Zachary Thomas, *Catholic World Report*, December 29, 2019, https://www.catholic worldreport.com/2019/12/29/cardinal-sarah-we-must-rebuild-the-cathedral -we-do-not-need-to-invent-a-new-church/. The excerpt is from a conference given by Cardinal Sarah at Église Saint François-Xavier in Paris, May 25, 2019, just hours after he visited the Cathedral of Notre-Dame of Paris. It was originally posted on *Catholic World Report* on June 21, 2019.

[5] Benedict, *The Rule of St. Benedict*, ed. Timothy Fry, O.S.B. (New York: Vintage Books, 1998), p. 13.

[6] Ibid., pp. 13–14.

number of conversions that would take place within our communities if we took seriously the call to radical hospitality, that "all guests who present themselves are to be welcomed as Christ."[7] Hospitality is not about keeping guests entertained but about offering an open heart and looking for God's presence in every person who comes through the door. Saint Benedict teaches us that if we close ourselves to the stranger, we close ourselves to the sacred. True hospitality—a tell-tale sign of any healthy community—is about loving one person at a time in the same way that God has first loved us.

Healthy community life is also built on a foundation of trust and integrity. We are called to give others the benefit of the doubt and fight against subcultures of suspicion. However, being trustworthy is not equivalent to being flawless. It simply means being worthy of trust. Therefore, Saint Benedict encourages us to repent of our faults as soon as we become aware of them and make amends immediately. It's also worth noting that transparency and consistent communication are powerful healing forces in any community, while the three greatest poisons are complaining, sarcasm, and gossip. To use our speech only to encourage, affirm, and show gratitude is a beautiful gift in community and an act of rare heroism in today's world. *repair*

On a related note, young people need to be led and formed by those who have gone before them. Therefore, mentorship is a key hallmark of any healthy community. From spiritual directors to professional mentors, those adults with experience in life should always be quick to share their wisdom and indeed their very lives with the next generation.

[7] Ibid., p. 51.

UNITY AND COMPLEMENTARITY

In one of his many agrarian tales, Wendell Berry writes from a first-person perspective about the life and times of a small-town barber named Jayber Crow. As an orphan and an outsider in Port William, Kentucky, Crow is painfully aware of the community and trust in the very root system of that small town. Long before he settled in Port William, he wandered through schools and jobs looking for his purpose in life. While still struggling with "hopelessness and sorrow" as a young man, he knew that he had to find his place in the world, somewhere he could come to "know the fundamental things".[8] Upon finding an inexplicable sense of belonging in Port William, he reflects:

> I just *felt* at home. After I got to Port William, I didn't feel any longer that I needed to look around to see if there was someplace I would like better. I quit wondering what I was going to make of myself. A lot of my doubts and questions were settled. You could say, I guess, that I was glad at last to be classified. I was not a preacher or a teacher or a student or a traveler. I was Port William's bachelor barber, and a number of satisfactions were available to me as the perquisites of that office.[9]

All of us share this deep need to feel at home, to belong to a place and share membership in a community. Without it, we'll forever be restless. We won't have a larger circle to invite others into nor have a context for thinking about key social principles like solidarity, subsidiarity, and the common good.

[8] Wendell Berry, *Jayber Crow* (Berkeley, CA: Counterpoint Press, 2001), p. 73.
[9] Ibid., p. 123.

While I've never lived in a small town, I've experienced the intimacy and joy of community life time and time again. From my one year at seminary to a decade of leading intentional homes for young adults in Nashville, I've seen countless conversions unfold and vocations discerned through community life rooted in the principles of this book. Whether it's a group of friends living under the same roof or a faithful family living a common way of life, we need physical places that empower us to live these principles until they spill over and shape culture all around us. On the flip side, I've seen young people on fire after summer camps and weekend retreats who slide back into their former ways of life within a matter of months. What was missing? They didn't have a profound sense of community at home or in their parishes. Conversion without community rarely lasts.

As diverse communities overlap with a spirit of unity and complementarity, they form the basis of a larger culture. As we all know, some individuals are particularly gifted with building and connecting communities and even shaping the larger culture. They are the "connectors" of the world according to author Malcolm Gladwell. They "manage to occupy many different worlds and subcultures and niches" all at once due to their unique combination of "curiosity, self-confidence, sociability, and energy".[10] He describes everyone from Kevin Bacon to Paul Revere as classic connectors who have a special gift of mobilizing others and bringing them together under a common cause. If that description fits you, you have an opportunity and responsibility to build community everywhere you go. Be bold and show the rest of us the way.

---

[10] Malcolm Gladwell, *The Tipping Point: How Little Things Can Make a Big Difference* (Boston: Back Bay Books/Little, Brown, 2019), pp. 48–49.

We're not all connectors, but we must all stay connected to each other lest we spiral into lives of isolation. Christ is the vine, and we are the branches (Jn 15:5). Our families, businesses, and apostolates are the only encounters that some people will ever have with the Gospel. We *have* to live the principle of community well to reach them and keep them in the fold. It's the logical result of *friendship*, the necessary safeguard of *mission*, and the building block of our final principle of *culture*. It's essential for those who intend to not only persevere in their faith but also spread the Gospel in our culture of noise.

What is holding us back, my dear friends? We have exactly what the world longs for in these dark and despairing times. Let's show them what true community rooted in Christ looks like.

GETTING PRACTICAL

- Beginning with your family, workplace, school, and church, do a quick assessment of your community right now. Where are the keys areas for improvement?
- Host a house concert, book club, or movie night to build community intentionally among your family, friends, coworkers, or neighbors.
- If you're not already, plug into a local parish. It's not enough just to show up on Sundays. Find a way to give back and invest in your local church community.
- Call your parents or sit them down over a meal just to say thank you for providing your first experience of community as a family growing up.
- Start a small group and read this book in community. Begin to apply these principles in your day-to-day life and hold others accountable to them as well.

FURTHER READING

Benedict. *The Rule of St. Benedict*. Edited by Timothy Fry, O.S.B. New York: Vintage Books, 1998.

Berry, Wendell. *Jayber Crow*. Berkeley, CA: Counterpoint Press, 2001.

Bonhoeffer, Dietrich. *Life Together*. Translated by Daniel W. Bloesch. Minneapolis: Fortress Press, 2015.

Lovasik, Lawrence G. *The Hidden Power of Kindness: A Practical Handbook for Souls Who Dare to Transform the World, One Deed at a Time*. Manchester, NH: Sophia Institute Press, 1999.

Nisbet, Robert A. *The Quest for Community: A Study in the Ethics of Order and Freedom*. Wilmington, DE: ISI Books, 1953.

Chapter 8

Suffering

ˈsəf(ə)riNG | *noun* | *the state of undergoing pain, distress, or hardship.*

It was a totally normal Monday morning in Nashville until I received an unexpected phone call from my dad. I had just returned home from morning Mass and had begun my usual workday out of my home office. I was a young entrepreneur at the time, finding ways to make a living through live events, music promotion, and real estate. My wheels were turning as they always did at the beginning of a new week, so the last thing I expected that morning was news of a family tragedy.

My dad and I used to chat weekly over the phone but never on a Monday morning. Between his work schedule and mine, that was the least likely time of the week for either of us to be available. When his name and number suddenly flashed on my phone, I immediately closed my office door and sat down at my desk. His voice was trembling on the other end of the line as he said, "Jimmy, your brother is gone." Initially, I was confused and wondered what he meant. He quickly explained that my brother, Bobby, had died in his sleep, and I was the first in the family to hear about it. Immediately, my whole world turned gray. I felt numb everywhere. Only when my dad asked me to find my sister and tell her in person did I finally snap out of the paralysis. I couldn't cry; I was in total shock.

Less than twenty minutes later, I found my sister on her way to class. We stood in the parking lot of a cathedral across the street from her college campus as I told her the gut-wrenching news. She collapsed into my arms, at which point the flood gates opened for both of us. We cried and hugged each other amid the pain and confusion. What else can be done in a moment filled with so much anguish? We had been with our brother on Thanksgiving only a few days prior, so it was impossible to understand how he could suddenly be gone. We quickly realized that we needed to drive home to be with our parents. We were both living in Nashville at the time, and our hometown of Atlanta was four hours away by car. We packed our bags, prayed with a priest who came to console us when he heard the news, and began the drive down to Atlanta.

Words cannot begin to describe the grief that compounded during the days leading up to Bobby's funeral. The sheer number of phone calls, emails, and texts offering condolences was overwhelming. My parents had been divorced for a few years, so it was also difficult knowing how best to console them while entering into my own grief. Much of my sorrow was initially felt through seeing the sadness of others. It was months before the shock wore off and I was able to begin my own process of healing.

There's nothing beautiful about suffering. It's ugly and painful. We encounter it all the time through the poverty, addiction, and misery of others. We encounter it in our own brokenness every day. We need to look no further than the Cross to verify that the worst suffering is at times gruesome. There's nothing easy about journeying with others in their agony or avoiding bitterness amid our own. And yet, the fruits of suffering, when united with Christ's, are beautiful beyond measure.

At the time of my brother's passing, I had heard the Church's teachings about redemptive suffering. I had contemplated our Lord's Passion and death enough times to know that suffering never had the final word. Yet, all the knowledge in the world meant nothing if it didn't sink into my heart and teach me how to suffer well. Having first read them in college, these words from Pope Benedict XVI in his encyclical *Spe Salvi* rang through my memory as I attempted to make sense of my brother's death:

> We can try to limit suffering, to fight against it, but we cannot eliminate it. It is when we attempt to avoid suffering by withdrawing from anything that might involve hurt, when we try to spare ourselves the effort and pain of pursuing truth, love, and goodness, that we drift into a life of emptiness, in which there may be almost no pain, but the dark sensation of meaninglessness and abandonment is all the greater. It is not by sidestepping or fleeing from suffering that we are healed, but rather by our capacity for accepting it, maturing through it and finding meaning through union with Christ, who suffered with infinite love.[1]

Benedict XVI further describes prayer and suffering as the two great schools for hope and the most effective means by which God expands our longing for heaven. When I look back with hindsight, it's clear that my brother's death gave me a whole new appreciation for life and taught me how to live with an eternal perspective. I have awakened with a certain intensity of purpose every day since, never wanting to waste a moment or take a single opportunity for granted.

Initially, these nuggets of wisdom didn't lessen the pain of losing Bobby. The suffering was not taken away by good

---

[1] Benedict XVI, *The Encyclicals of Benedict XVI* (London: Catholic Truth Society, 2013), p. 89.

theology, but rather it was given a profound sense of purpose. Even before I could see the long-term fruits, I knew that God would bring good out of the evil of my brother's passing. Not only that, but he could bring an even greater good out of it than might have been possible otherwise. There's no better example of this than "the greatest moral evil ever committed—the rejection and murder of God's only Son" that brought about "the greatest of goods: the glorification of Christ and our redemption".[2] These words from the *Catechism of the Catholic Church* defend this great paradox, as do the lives and stories of countless saints. God is endlessly creative and generous in his work of transforming evil into good and suffering into beauty.

Look at Job in the Old Testament, whose fidelity to the Lord was tested to the point of losing everything and (almost) everyone he loved. Still, he was able to declare, "Naked I came from my mother's womb, and naked shall I return; the LORD gave, and the LORD has taken away; blessed be the name of the LORD" (1:21). Ponder the words of Saint Paul, who reminds us to "rejoice in [our] sufferings" and "complete what is lacking in Christ's afflictions for the sake of his body, that is, the church" (Col 1:24). There's great dignity in suffering well. It's also the source of our most deep-seated redemption and sanctification.

SUFFERING THAT SANCTIFIES

The hail pounded on us as we continued a several-mile hike through a glorious mountain range in central Wyoming. We were many thousands of feet above sea level, and it felt like we were standing in the middle of a storm cloud.

---

[2] *Catechism of the Catholic Church*, no. 312.

Optimism was running low, and cynicism had taken hold of our hearts as we searched for shelter and safety. There were twenty of us on this backcountry adventure in the summer of 2021 and to top it off, we were lost. We had already crisscrossed a section of the mountain a few times looking for a solid footpath that would lead us to our campsite for the night.

In the height of the frustration and fatigue, an old line from Saint John of Ávila rose to the surface of my memory, and I shouted, "One 'Blessed be God' in times of adversity is worth more than a thousand acts of gratitude in times of prosperity!"[3] I had read the line many times before, but it suddenly meant more to me than ever. Slowly, "Blessed be God" became our communal chant as we persevered through the elements and waited for the weather to die down. Joy slowly overtook all of us, and before I knew it, the chant gave way to off-and-on singing for several hours. The hail eventually stopped, and we found our footpath. But nothing could quite describe the satisfaction we had found along the way.

The joy of denying our will (or better yet, of uniting it with God's will) is a great mystery. More specifically, when we unite our suffering with the Cross, we assist Jesus in his great mission of redemption. We help him save souls, which is the very meaning of the Church's teaching on redemptive suffering.[4] It's a powerful source of apostolic joy. According to Father Jean C.J. d'Elbée in his self-guided retreat *I Believe in Love*, "The money

---

[3] John of Ávila, cited in Alfonso Maria de' Liguori, *Uniformity with God's Will*, trans. Thomas W. Tobin, C.Ss.R. (Charlotte, NC: TAN Books, 2013), p. 8.

[4] John Paul II, Apostolic Letter on the Christian Meaning of Human Suffering *Salvifici Doloris* (February 11, 1984), no. 17, https://www.vatican.va /content/john-paul-ii/en/apost_letters/1984/documents/hf_jp-ii_apl_11021 984_salvifici-doloris.html.

to buy souls is suffering, accepted with love."[5] Every single day, from the smallest pinpricks that we offer up to the greatest sufferings that we surrender, we're never more helpful in God's redemption of the human race than when we unite our suffering with his on the Cross. Father d'Elbée further reflects:

> Think of all those for whom you purchase eternal bliss by a suffering which is, after all, transitory. Suffering is a gold-mine to exploit for saving souls, for helping missionaries, for being a hidden apostle. What happiness it is to be able to suffer when we cannot act![6]

While tremendous suffering has great redemptive power, even the smallest annoyances properly united with the Cross can sanctify us and save others. For example, every effort to curb our inclination to complain when something doesn't go our way is a powerful act of mortification. Saint Alphonsus de Liguori goes so far as to say that wishing for better weather on an unbearably hot day or even in the middle of a hailstorm indicates "opposition to God's will" and that we should instead be content for "things to be just as they are".[7] According to this divine logic, we should never prefer health over sickness, comfort over poverty, or ease over hardship. Nothing is wasted in the light of redemption, even the smallest of human adversities.

[5] Jean du Coeur de Jésus d'Elbée, *I Believe in Love: A Personal Retreat Based on the Teaching of St. Thérèse of Lisieux* (Manchester, NH: Sophia Institute Press, 2001), p. 195. This edition includes minor revisions to the original text: trans. Marilyn Teichert and Madeleine Stebbins, originally published in Chicago in 1974 by Franciscan Herald Press.

[6] Ibid., p. 203.

[7] De' Liguori, *Uniformity with God's Will*, pp. 17–18.

In suffering well, we not only help Jesus save souls but also give him an opportunity to sanctify us. According to C. S. Lewis in *The Problem of Pain*, the whole purpose of suffering is to teach us how to deny our will so we can unite it to the Father's will:

> The redemptive effect of suffering lies chiefly in its tendency to reduce the rebel will. Ascetic practices, which in themselves strengthen the will, are only useful in so far as they enable the will to put its own house (the passions) in order, as a preparation for offering the whole man to God. They are necessary as a means; as an end, they would be abominable, for in substituting will for appetite and there stopping, they would merely exchange the animal self for the diabolical self. It was, therefore, truly said that "only God can mortify"....
>
> Hence the Perfect Man brought to Gethsemane a will, and a strong will, to escape suffering and death if such escape were compatible with the Father's will, combined with a perfect readiness for obedience if it were not.[8]

Suffering does violence to our "rebel will" and heals our stubbornness that so often controls our reactions to disappointment, frustration, and great pain. There's so much power in surrendering our suffering to Jesus at its very onset, in clinging to him who knows what we need better than we do. Whether it's self-imposed suffering such as fasting and mortification or unforeseeable suffering like the death of a loved one, it all carries great potential for uniting our will with the Father's and furthering our Lord's work of redemption. In the final analysis, joy follows suffering because the Resurrection follows the Cross. God

[8] C. S. Lewis, *The Problem of Pain* (San Francisco: HarperCollins, 1996), pp. 112–13.

can use even the most agonizing of trials and tragedies for his greater glory.

FROM SUFFERING TO COMPASSION

Several years ago, I led a three-day parish mission in Florida that was filled with countless graces. I remember feeling unworthy to proclaim the Gospel to so many beautiful people as I shared aspects of my personal testimony each night. It had been only three years since my brother's death, and the healing that followed became a central theme that touched the hearts of many going through similar suffering and loss. I pointed out that the shared grief of my parents had reconciled them after several years of being divorced. I talked about my sister's sorrow that taught her to cling to the Lord as never before, strengthening her faith and leading her into her vocation. She's now married with a beautiful, growing family. I shared about my own experience of healing in Adoration several months after Bobby's passing and the profound calling to be an older brother in the lives of young people that came with it.

What began as a deep wound in my heart was healing and already becoming a fountain of life for others. To borrow imagery from Hans Urs von Balthasar in *Heart of the World*, the Holy Spirit had slowly moved me out of the "wilderness" into the "realm of miracles" where there is nothing but "gardens, fountains, birds ... [and] sheer truth".[9] Life was overcoming death in my soul, and God was inviting me to share that truth and promise with others.

[9] Hans Urs von Balthasar, *Heart of the World* (San Francisco: Ignatius Press, 1979), p. 158.

By the third day of the parish mission, I had several appointments set up at a local coffee shop. Always unexpected and cherished, these one-on-one meetings usually happened as a result of a small moment in a talk that struck a chord with someone. A brief conversation would ensue at the end of the night, and a meeting over coffee would be scheduled for the next day. These more intimate conversations were highlights of the parish mission.

As I walked into the coffee shop just after lunchtime, the first brave soul wanting to meet hurriedly caught my attention. Before I knew it, I was sitting down with a middle-aged gentleman of utter sincerity and kindness. His eyes were already welling up with tears as he offered me my first cup of coffee for the afternoon. Moments later, he was inviting me into the greatest suffering of his life: the death of his wife three years prior. There was little that could be said in response to his captivating stories of romance, family, and tragedy. Here was a man that knew what it meant to give his heart away in love. He knew the joy of self-emptying and the grief of losing what one cares for the most. And for three years, a dark cloud had enveloped him. The heartbreak and confusion of losing his wife seemed just as raw now as it had on the day of her passing. At this moment, all he needed was someone to talk to, some assurance that he was not alone in his suffering, and that grace could be found in the darkness. Before I knew it, an hour had passed and we were closing our time together in prayer.

A few minutes later, a young man in high school walked through the door, eager to meet for the second time that week. Having spent time together at a camp in the summertime, he was already like a younger brother to me. With a similar temperament and a spiritual life mature beyond his years, he was a great consolation and encouragement. To see purity and holiness in the life of a young person was a great joy, and we sat for quite some time that day sharing heavenly inspirations and hopes. It was the kind of conversation that comes naturally only in a virtuous friendship. It became clear by the end of this second meeting that God simply wanted to remind us both of how profoundly he delights in us.

Nothing could have prepared me for the third and final meeting that afternoon. As is so often the case when God is on the move, this one started late and had a few unexpected turns. A young man early in his college career walked in with his two recently divorced parents. He did not live close enough to take part in the three-day parish mission but had driven specifically into town that day to have coffee. We, too, had met at a camp that previous summer, where we had separately experienced powerful, life-changing weeks. Since I knew at least part of his story, I had been praying for him ever since.

I was initially surprised when he walked in with his parents. Thinking that our one-on-one time had quickly become a family affair, I started pulling up extra chairs at our table while exchanging brief pleasantries with his parents. They soon motioned to each other and moved together toward the opposite end of the room with coffee in hand. They had planned all along to spend some time together just the two of them, and to my knowledge, this was their first peaceful encounter in over a year. As they walked away, I felt humbled to know more of their story than they did of mine. I felt joy in seeing the first inklings of what appeared to be real forgiveness.

As I sat down with their son, my heart was already full of compassion. It had become clear to me at camp that this young man was self-aware beyond his years and transparent

to a fault. Though he had many struggles, goodness radi-
ated through his eyes. Over the next hour and a half, he
proceeded to tell me of his ongoing drug addictions and
promiscuous lifestyle since being in college. He shared
his struggles to keep up with constantly mounting school
work. He had been away from church and far from prayer
since our last conversation. Depression seemed to him a
dark and ever-present abyss.

His vulnerability and brokenness moved me. It shook
me in the deepest place of who I am. After spending most
of the time listening, I found a moment of silence and
burst into a passionate monologue about God's love for
him. It felt as if my heart was going to explode, as if the
grace of God was opening up through me and pouring
into the heart of this young man. None of the words spo-
ken felt like my own, and quickly his eyes ran with tears.
The deepest longings of his heart were being touched by
God's love, and you could sense a certain peace and healing
around him for several minutes. Even without articulating
it, he knew he was loved at that moment. Before long,
we were closing our time in prayer, and his parents were
walking the length of the coffee shop to say goodbye. As
they walked out the door, peace and healing surrounded
me as well. I, too, had desperately needed to hear those
words of love and affection from my heavenly Father.

When suffering leads to wounds and those wounds are
healed over time, our hearts overflow with compassion.
We cannot help but love those who are furthest away from
the Lord. We burn with zeal for the sheep who has left the
fold and cannot wait to reunite him with the other ninety-
nine (Mt 18:12–14; Lk 15:3–7). This is what it means to
suffer with others and lead them to God who suffered for
love of us all. This is what true compassion is all about.

SIGN OF GOD'S LOVE

It cannot be said enough: we are deeply and fervently loved, most especially in our suffering. Knowing this truth and believing it is the answer to one of the greatest questions of the human heart. The more we surrender our suffering to God and allow him to heal our wounds, the more they will become fountains of life for others. All pain feels like hell in the moment, but the only real hell is no longer being able to love. Because we are created in the image of God, who is a communion of Love, our hearts are restless until they rest in him who suffered to the point of death. The earliest Christians were martyred for this saving doctrine. The reality is that our own suffering can take many different forms—grief, betrayal, sickness, loneliness, pain, uncertainty—but all of it makes us more like Christ if we unite it to his Cross.

There are few things our post-Christian culture is more afraid of than suffering. Without an eternal perspective, suffering is totally meaningless. Without faith, it has no redemptive power. In the words of Bishop Fulton Sheen, it's a tragedy to think of all the wasted suffering in today's faithless world:

> What is mysterious is not the suffering but how much is missed when we do suffer! Think of all the feverish brows in hospitals who cannot sanctify that pain by correlating it to Our Lord with a crown of thorns. Think of the wounded who could sanctify their wounds if they only knew how, by correlating them in some way with Hands that were riven with nails. Think of all the aching hearts with worries, anxieties, and fears who could bear the cross if they only loved a Heart that was opened by a lance.[10]

[10] Fulton Sheen, *Life Is Worth Living* (San Francisco: Ignatius Press, 1999), p. 270.

Suffering is senseless until we realize how God allows it to draw us close to himself and remind us that we are strangers and sojourners made for him alone. At times his mercy is severe, doing whatever it takes to detach us from the things of this world and unite us with him. As we grow in our relationship with God, the tension of the "already but not yet" can be anguish for the soul. We may *already* be in a place of great intimacy with him, but we're *not yet* in the fullness of Love that awaits us in heaven. Even this is a source of great suffering for the soul in love with God.

I'm reminded of the nuptial cry of Adam, that blessed moment when he realized that man was not meant to be alone. He beheld Eve for the first time and cried, "Bone of my bones and flesh of my flesh" (Gen 2:23). These words ring true every time the human heart falls in love. We are made for more, even when we cannot see how. These words also ring true every time we enter into our suffering with great trust in the Father's loving providence. Courage fills our hearts, for our Divine Lover is calling out to us and inviting us to follow him in his Passion and death.

These great mysteries of God's sacrificial love are the bedrock of Christian faith. To believe that God's suffering is at the heart of what it means to be human is quintessential Christian doctrine. To believe that he knit us together in our mother's womb (Ps 139:13) and died for us on the Cross is a sign of grace already at work in our lives. Indeed, what a marvelous mystery that God has been passionately pursuing us from the moment he created us! His original design was simple: that we would have no fear of being unloved and no shame in giving ourselves away, even unto death. We once walked with God in the cool breeze of the garden and ruled over all the earth in perfect harmony with each other and the land. One day we shall rule again;

in dying to ourselves and surrendering to his love, we will be more than conquerors.

It's a great paradox to think that suffering makes us more human, increasing our capacity for compassion and intimacy with others. It's also the surest pathway to victory in the Christian life. Look at Saint Maximilian Kolbe, Saint Gemma Galgani, Saint Lawrence, or any of the great saints of history. Their narrow ways into heaven were always in the shape of a cross. Though we may not experience their physical torment or dark nights of the soul, all of us must pass through suffering if we are to arrive at our own resurrection.

Let us not be afraid to fall in love with God, who poured out every last drop of his blood on the Cross. He loves us beyond our wildest imagination. Let us be fearless before the hard reality of suffering, for this is our freedom and glory as children of God! May we enter into his wounds and remain steadfast along our way to Calvary.

GETTING PRACTICAL

- Say, "Blessed be God," every time you're tempted to complain. Accept the smallest annoyances and even the most difficult circumstances of your day as a gift from God.
- The next time you're confronted with some great trial or tragedy, immediately unite it with our Lord on the Cross. In prayer, ask the Holy Spirit to help you find seeds of the resurrection amid the suffering.
- Commit to some form of self-denial every day, even if it's as simple as skipping dessert. Find little ways to mortify your "rebel will" and unite it with the Cross.
- Look for opportunities to be with others amid their suffering. Reach out to those who you know are going

through a difficult time with a phone call or an invitation to dinner.

- Pray the Sorrowful Mysteries of the Rosary at least twice a week, ideally on Tuesdays and Fridays.

FURTHER READING

Benedict XVI. Encyclical Letter on Christian Hope *Spe Salvi*. November 30, 2007. https://www.vatican.va /content/benedict-xvi/en/encyclicals/documents/hf _ben-xvi_enc_20071130_spe-salvi.html.

Frankl, Viktor E. *Man's Search for Meaning*. Part one translated by Ilse Lasch. Boston: Beacon Press, 2006.

John Paul II. Apostolic Letter on the Christian Meaning of Human Suffering *Salvifici Doloris*. February 11, 1984. https://www.vatican.va/content/john-paul-ii/en /apost_letters/1984/documents/hf_jp-ii_apl_1102 1984_salvifici-doloris.html.

Kreeft, Peter. *Making Sense Out of Suffering*. Ann Arbor, MI: Servant Books, 1986.

Lewis, C. S. *The Problem of Pain*. New York: HarperOne, 2015.

Vanauken, Sheldon. *A Severe Mercy*. London: Hodder & Stoughton, 2011.

Chapter 9

Mission

'miSHən | noun | a strongly felt aim, ambition, or calling.

Seven months after my brother's sudden passing, I was in the north Georgia mountains leading a summer camp for a few hundred high schoolers. I was only a few miles away from where my own deepening conversion had occurred while in high school, but I had not yet fully grieved or recovered from the recent family tragedy. It seemed like miracles had unfolded all around me, particularly for my parents and sister, but I was still angry with God and resentful toward my brother. I couldn't understand why he had to die so young or why we had never been as close as I had always wanted to be. I needed God not just to heal me but to give me a new heart. The words of the prophet Ezekiel could not have been more appealing: "A new heart I will give you, and a new spirit I will put within you; and I will take out of your flesh the heart of stone and give you a heart of flesh" (36:26). It was high time for healing and hope to propel my life forward.

The night before camp ended that week, several hundred of us gathered for Eucharistic Adoration. I spent much of the week giving talks and preparing everyone to encounter the Lord during this night of prayer, and I realized quickly how much I needed my own encounter with him. Halfway into Adoration, I noticed two young men toward the front of the room. The one who was slightly older whispered to the other, "I love you, brother." It was barely audible, but it stood out in a powerful way because those were words I had never heard growing up. Fifteen minutes later, I noticed the same two young men. This time, the older one placed his hand on the shoulder of the younger one, clearly praying for him and interceding for him. Suddenly, I felt a hand on the back of my shoulder. I never turned around to see who it was, but something deep inside me knew that God was at work. This brief moment of brotherly intercessory prayer moved me. I decided to surrender all my pain, and I knew that God was on the move. I just didn't understand how yet.

The next day as we were all saying our goodbyes, a chaperone from Texas walked up to me and said, "I know this is going to sound a little crazy, but that was my hand on your shoulder last night in Adoration. I really believe that God asked me to put it there, and he wants you to know a few things. He wants you to know that your brother loves you, that he's proud of you, and that he wants me to call you 'Jimbo' from this point forward." Nothing could have prepared me for this conversation. Immediately, I felt a rush of healing and forgiveness, and an immense weight lifted off my shoulders. I suddenly felt closer to Bobby than I had ever felt to him during his earthly life. As I took that conversation to prayer over the next several weeks, God made it very clear that he not only brought about a great healing in my heart that day, but he also confirmed a great calling: to be an older brother in the lives of young people that my brother had not been able to be for me. Over the next ten years, I traveled the world several times over to be faithful to that calling and to convince as many young people as possible of the Father's love for them.

Though I'm traveling less these days, the joy of this mission continues to deepen and unfold. It's clear to me that the greatest callings in life are born out of the greatest sufferings. Look at every great prophet in the Old Testament; look at every great apostle in the New. God is in the business of healing our wounds, piercing them with his love, and transforming them into beautiful fountains of life for others. This mysterious truth is evident in the lives of all the greatest saints. It's evident in the lives of ordinary Christians as well.

UNIVERSAL BUT UNIQUE

While the universal call to holiness can be traced to both the Old and the New Testament, and had been recalled by great spiritual writers like Saint Francis de Sales and Saint Josemaría Escrivá, it was not given particular prominence in the Church's teachings until the Second Vatican Council over half a century ago. Promulgated in 1964, the dogmatic constitution *Lumen Gentium* declared that every Christian across every state of life is called to holiness:

> Thus it is evident to everyone, that all the faithful of Christ of whatever rank or status, are called to the fullness of the Christian life and to the perfection of charity; by this holiness as such a more human manner of living is promoted in this earthly society. In order that the faithful may reach this perfection, they must use their strength accordingly as they have received it, as a gift from Christ. They must follow in His footsteps and conform themselves to His image seeking the will of the Father in all

things. They must devote themselves with all their being
to the glory of God and the service of their neighbor.
In this way, the holiness of the People of God will grow
into an abundant harvest of good, as is admirably shown
by the life of so many saints in Church history.[1]

For a long time, there was an assumption among some
Catholics that only priests and religious were called to holiness. Up until the release of *Lumen Gentium*, many thought
that there was little opportunity for the laity to become great
saints. In contrast, many of today's young Catholics have
heard this call to holiness and have responded to it gener-
ously. In the same way that Christ called every one of his
disciples to holiness, Catholics across every state of life (like
other Christians across many denominations) are waking up
to the Lord's call to holiness here and now. Why not take
him at his word when he unequivocally calls each of us to
be "perfect, as [our] heavenly Father is perfect" (Mt 5:48)?

However, what is still often missing in the Church is a
radical embrace of the universal call to *mission*. We need to
return to the dynamism of the early Church, whereby "the
laity—as individuals, families, and entire communities—
shared in spreading the faith."[2] These words of Saint John
Paul II do not relegate the work of evangelization to priests
and religious, but rather empower the laity to stand on the
front lines of the Church's great battle for souls. Each of
us has a part to play in the great mission of our Redeemer.
His mission is our mission, which is nothing less than the
redemption of the entire human race.

---

[1] Second Vatican Council, Dogmatic Constitution on the Church *Lumen
Gentium* (November 21, 1964), no. 40, https://www.vatican.va/archive/hist
_councils/ii_vatican_council/documents/vat-ii_const_19641121_lumen
-gentium_en.html.

[2] John Paul II, *Encyclical Letter "Redemptoris Missio" on the Permanent Validity of
the Church's Missionary Mandate* (Boston: Pauline Books & Media, 1999), p. 90.

Because I had so many evangelical friends in college who were zealous for the salvation of souls, I learned early on how to be bold in sharing the Gospel. Their fervor became my own. Toward the beginning of my senior year at Vanderbilt, I came across Saint John Paul II's great encyclical *Mission of the Redeemer*, which confirmed my growing suspicion that evangelization wasn't just for religious missionaries but a mandate for every baptized soul. We cannot escape it. It's built into our baptismal calling. Our lives are meant to proclaim the Gospel. That, in summary, is the entire goal of this book. While art, music, and books are powerful tools for evangelization, our way of life is how beauty evangelizes best.

By the grace of God, each of us has a unique and unrepeatable way of living our life mission and of evangelizing our culture of noise. It looks different for all of us based on our vocation, season of life, and concrete circumstances. According to Saint John Paul II in his apostolic exhortation *Christifideles Laici* about the mission of the laity, God sees and calls each one of us differently:

> In fact, from eternity God has thought of us and has loved us as unique individuals. Every one of us he called by name, as the Good Shepherd "calls his sheep by name" (Jn 10:3). However, only in the unfolding of the history of our lives and its events is the eternal plan of God revealed to each of us. Therefore, it is a gradual process; in a certain sense, one that happens day by day.[3]

For those of you who are called to the priesthood, your mission is great—whether it be thousands of families under

[3] John Paul II, Post-Synodal Apostolic Exhortation on the Vocation and the Mission of the Lay Faithful in the Church and in the World *Christifideles Laici* (December 30, 1988), no. 58, https://www.vatican.va/content/john-paul-ii /en/apost_exhortations/documents/hf_jp-ii_exh_30121988_christifideles-laici .html.

your spiritual fatherhood at a parish or hundreds of souls entrusted to your care at a school. For those who are called to religious life, your primary mission is found in your constitution. You are called above all to storm heaven with your brothers or sisters in religious life and to sanctify others every step of the way. For the vast majority who are called to family life, your primary mission is to lead your spouse and children to heaven. Secondarily, you have a great opportunity to bring the Gospel to your neighbors, coworkers, friends, and extended family. This extended mission is even greater for those who are single and have a radical availability to souls around them. Until entering the fullness of your vocation, those who are single have a great responsibility to be generous with the Lord in reaching out to others through the apostolate of friendship.

How is God calling you on mission? In what ways does your vocation (or your future vocation) shape your response to this universal call to help Jesus save souls? Your mission will naturally flow out of your fidelity to our eight previous principles. However, now is a great opportunity to take stock of your gifts, limitations, and circumstances. God's calling in your life may be very apostolic, like becoming a priest or working full-time for the Church. It may be very subtle, like bringing the Gospel into otherwise secular environments like business, politics, and medicine. But *it all matters* because it's all part of our Lord's great mission of redemption.

The key is to discern well, for we each have an irreplaceable part to play in the salvation of souls. There is no greater tool for this discernment than the rules found in *The Spiritual Exercises of St. Ignatius of Loyola.*[4] However, I

[4] A good resource is Timothy M. Gallagher, O.M.V., *The Discernment of Spirits: An Ignatian Guide for Everyday Living* (New York: Crossroad Publishing, 2005).

recently came across a simple summary of spiritual discernment by contemplative author Father Wilfrid Stinissen, which provides a strong starting place for those seeking God's will in their lives:

1. Inspirations from the Holy Spirit always align with the Gospel. If we can't back up a decision with a solid basis in Christ's life and teachings, then we're in trouble.

2. God's will is always reasonable, having a strong foundation in prudence and human wisdom.

3. Inspirations from the Holy Spirit always bring lasting peace and joy, even if they sometimes begin with a certain restlessness.

4. God's will never makes excessive demands nor does it create heavy burdens. It acknowledges our human limitations and fosters humility.

5. Inspirations from the Holy Spirit are always rooted in reality. Any ideas that lead to endless dreams or fantasies are never from the Lord.

6. God's will is always rooted in the Church, with great love for her teachings and authority.[5]

The art of discerning one's mission in life (and ultimately one's vocation) must be rooted in prayer, experience, and ongoing spiritual direction. For me personally, the Lord has had me on mission for a long time. I suspect that one day there will be a profound integration between this missionary impulse and my permanent vocation. In the meantime, I have total confidence that he has called me to be faithful to his will here and now. And that

[5] Wilfrid Stinissen, O.C.D., *The Holy Spirit, Fire of Divine Love*, trans. Sister Clare Marie, O.C.D. (San Francisco: Ignatius Press, 2017), pp. 83–92.

confidence is rooted in fifteen years of daily prayer, lived experience, and regular spiritual direction.

THE ART OF ACCOMPANIMENT

Regardless of our personal mission or lifelong vocation, our zeal for souls must be rooted in a *cura personalis*, or care for the individual person. There's nothing less effective than street-corner preaching, door-to-door evangelization, or classroom catechesis that's forced and awkward. In the words of Saint Paul VI, "Modern man listens more willingly to witnesses than to teachers, and if he does listen to teachers, it is because they are witnesses."[6] Indeed, we must witness to the faith—deeply and personally—before attempting to invite others into it. Long before we preach the Gospel, we must acknowledge the humanity of others and love them as God has first loved us.

To put it another way, the Church needs experts in the art of accompaniment, those who take off their sandals before the hallowed ground of others and join them on pilgrimage with Christ to the Father.[7] Without the love of God fueling us, accompanying others is a hollow endeavor that inspires cults of personality rather than the worship of God. We don't want to lead people to ourselves but to the Lord. Without the Church and her sacraments, our apostolic fruits do not endure. What we need is disinterested

[6] Paul VI, Apostolic Exhortation on Evangelization in the Modern World *Evangelii Nuntiandi* (December 8, 1975), no. 41, quoting his Address to the Members of the Consilium de Laicis (October 2, 1974), https://www.vatican.va/content/paul-vi/en/apost_exhortations/documents/hf_p-vi_exh_19751208_evangelii-nuntiandi.html.

[7] Francis, *Evangelii Gaudium: The Joy of the Gospel* (New York: Image, 2014), pp. 120–21.

and generous love for others that leads them to abundant life with Christ and his Church.

The opening line of our Lord in the Gospel of John reveals the starting place for any great mission: "What do you seek?" Jesus asks Andrew as he looks at him with great love (1:38). Andrew stumbles around for an answer but eventually realizes that this is the fundamental question of his life. What does he desire? What is his heart really after? We have to begin every apostolic endeavor with the same question and the same look of love. Pope Benedict XVI once wrote, "I can give to others much more than their outward necessities; I can give them the look of love which they crave."[8] What does it look like to love others with the heart of Christ? How do we ask them the most fundamental questions without being unnatural or forced? How do we know when they are ready to set aside surface-level wants and uncover their bottomless desire for God?

We can look to the lives of Saint John Bosco, Saint John Paul II, and countless other saints to learn how to love others so intensely that they cannot help but encounter Jesus. As we've already discovered in our previous principle of *prayer*, it all begins with our personal holiness as we help the Lord win souls every day on our knees. From the overflow of that prayer comes our genuine love that surprises others with joy. Before long, they begin asking all the right questions and are ready for a personal encounter with Jesus, who is the fulfillment of all their desires.

Once our prayer life is consistent, how can we provide such encounters with the Lord Jesus Christ? The answer is the Word of God and the sacraments. Without Sacred Scripture and the sacramental life of the Church, it is easy

---

[8] Benedict XVI, *The Encyclicals of Benedict XVI* (London: Catholic Truth Society, 2013), p. 25.

for evangelization never to move beyond the evangelist. Only through the Church can we provide tangible,
ongoing encounters with Jesus, who is radically present in
every confession and at every Mass. There are few greater
victories in the mission field than helping others make a
good confession or inspiring them to develop a love for
daily Mass.

Even as we root ourselves in prayer and point others to Christ's presence in the sacraments, it's imperative
that our "missionary style" focus "on the essentials, on
what is most beautiful, most grand, most appealing and
at the same time most necessary".[9] These words of Pope
Francis, written in his first apostolic exhortation *Evangelii
Gaudium,* go on to describe the "beauty of the saving love
of God made manifest in Jesus Christ who died and rose
from the dead" as the most essential truth of Christianity.[10] Because we're living in an apostolic age in which
the vast majority of people do not know the Gospel, this
foundational doctrine of redemption is what they need to
hear most. For the New Evangelization to sweep across
every land and across every charism, institution, and apostolate of the Church, it must be rooted in the beauty of
God's love found on the Cross.

After encountering Jesus and spending the day with
him, Andrew immediately told his brother Simon Peter
and "brought him to Jesus" (Jn 1:42). The simplicity and
significance of this moment cannot be overstated. Peter
goes on to become the rock upon which the Church is
built (Mt 16:18), all because his brother Andrew intro-
duced him to Jesus. How can we help others encounter
Jesus personally and give them the courage to chase after

---

[9] Francis, *Evangelii Gaudium,* p. 30.
[10] Ibid.

him with all their heart, mind, soul, and strength? With our selfless love and constant prayer, God can do anything.

With notable exceptions, much of the evangelization in the early Church took place one person at a time. Early Christians fostered a culture of accompaniment even amid widespread persecution, captivating family members and friends with the joy of the Gospel and courageously baptizing them one by one. Similarly, our steady witness and loving proclamation of the Gospel may be the only invitation some people ever receive to salvation. Now is the time. God is calling us by name.

THE GOD OF SURPRISES

Up until a few years ago, my life consisted of year-round conferences, retreats, and parish missions all over the world. When I wasn't traveling as an itinerant speaker, I was working out of Nashville with talented artists, musicians, and authors dedicated to the evangelization of culture through beauty. I spent all my free time mentoring young people in faith and virtue. As fear of the coronavirus cancelled every event on my calendar beginning in March 2020, I began hosting livestream retreats and concerts that were initially very fruitful. As a naturally optimistic person, I kept looking for the silver linings of the pandemic, but I was growing restless behind screens and cameras. I was feeling more isolated by the day. For a variety of reasons, I began thinking that God was calling me away from the evangelization and formation of young people. It was one of those areas of life where work and mission came together seamlessly, especially when I was on the road speaking at youth events. However, I began making plans for full-time entrepreneurship instead.

As this inner restlessness grew, I came across a Scripture passage from the prophet Isaiah and knew that it was time to "remember not the former things, nor consider the things of old" (43:18). I sensed that the Lord wanted to do something radically new in me, and so I wrote that passage down on a postcard and taped it to my bathroom mirror. A few weeks later, I received a phone call that changed my life. On the other end of the line was a great priest-friend offering me a dream job that I wasn't looking for. He wanted me to move to Tampa, Florida, and become director of campus ministry at an all-boys Jesuit high school. Having helped lead many of their retreats and pilgrimages through the years, I already had a great love for the school and its students. While it felt crazy to consider such a drastic life transition, my heart burst out of my chest at the mere thought of it. After a week of prayer and deliberation, I called the priest back to accept the job and moved three weeks later on the Feast of Saint Ignatius of Loyola.

Within the first few weeks of the school year, I knew that God was confirming my life mission of being an older brother in the lives of young people. Soon, a group of students and I started an after-school Rosary that has been consistent ever since. Daily Mass attendance grew steadily in the first semester. By springtime, twenty-two students became Catholic through our RCIA (Rite of Christian Initiation of Adults) program. It's clear that the culture of conversion on our campus is only growing by the day. Our school is a pocket of holiness in a world that's increasingly hostile to Christian faith. And my work in campus ministry and school administration has brought me more joy than I could have ever anticipated. What began as a working sabbatical in Florida has become the fullest expression of my life mission yet and the beginning of a lifelong career shift. God is indeed full of surprises.

This principle of *mission* is the natural overflow of all the other principles and the final cornerstone for our culminating principle of *culture*. It's a universal call with a unique application in every Christian's life. Regardless of the particulars, finding our life mission is integral to the art of being human. At the end of the day, we all stand unworthily with Saint Peter and the other disciples as our Lord calls us to "put out into the deep and let down [our] nets for a catch" (Lk 5:4). All of us have nets to cast and fishing lines to sink. The great mission of redemption continues with every generation, and we may contribute a catch. What will your mission be?

I'll leave you with the formidable words of Father Jesús Urteaga Loidi in his difficult-to-find book *Man, the Saint:*

> If you are one of those who launch out into the deep, set the helm straight and firmly, and let your motto be rather to die than turn back. If you give yourself to God give yourself like the saints did. Let no one and nothing occupy your attention and slow you down: you belong to God. If you give yourself, give yourself for eternity. Let neither the roaring waves nor the treacherous undercurrent shake the cement of your foundations. God depends on you: He leans on you. Put all your energy into it and row against the current.

> If you are gambling with sanctity, then stake your whole life on it. If you give everything, do not keep back your youth which is the most pleasant of all in the eyes of your Father. Boats and nets, dirty or torn, God will accept them if only you give them cheerfully.

> If, on the high seas, as you row along, you come across a corpse or two who groan of despair and desertion: keep on rowing, with your eyes fixed on heaven, and let the dead bury their dead. If the nights at sea are cold and dark, kiss the waters of that sea, and you will get comfort from

the heat of those who died on the way. If the lonely eve-
nings make you afraid, lift up your arms to heaven and the
wind will be your friend. If the thick fog of the long days
at sea lessens your youthful enthusiasm, shout to the waves
and you will see all the other boats which are going in the
same direction.

You will learn with time to read the stars and will see
that on your innermost parts words will begin to engrave
themselves: "Let down your nets for a catch." You will
recall the excuse that rose to the lips of St. Peter: "Master,
we have toiled all night, and caught nothing." Before God
has time to say anything you finish with the words of the
apostle: "At thy word I will let down the net." You will
cast it and the miracle will happen. You will call the others
to help you pull in the nets. And the Lord, who is there
in your boat, will smile, but it is your own arms that will
do the work. The laughter will change to tears when the
nets break, and you will look at Christ. Then God will
lend a hand. The word "miracle, miracle" will travel from
boat to boat, wafted by the wind softly over the waves,
and slowly reach the shore. "Miracle"—putting to shame
more than ever those who did not dare.

Duc in altum. Launch out into the deep waters with the
help of Christ's other lovers. What are we afraid of, men
of little faith?[11]

GETTING PRACTICAL

- Spend some time praying through the rules of discernment found in *The Spiritual Exercises of St. Ignatius of
  Loyola.* Begin tracing your own rhythm of consola-
  tions and desolations, taking note of how God calls you
  through sustained peace and joy.

[11] Jesús Urteaga Loidi, *Man, the Saint* (Fort Collins, CO: Roman Catholic
Books, 1960), pp. 130–31.

- Find a spiritual director who can help you listen to the Holy Spirit. Meet more frequently during seasons of intense discernment and decision-making.
- Commit to a local apostolate that requires a weekly commitment, whether it's volunteering at a soup kitchen or helping lead a youth group.
- Pray nightly for the five souls in your life who are most in need of Jesus. Then, go out of your way to love them until you've earned the right to share the Gospel.
- Go on a mission trip to get inspired by people who are responding radically to God's call in their lives. We often need prophetic witnesses to shake us out of our complacency.

FURTHER READING

Chautard, Jean-Baptiste, O.C.S.O. *The Soul of the Apostolate.* Translated by a monk of Our Lady of Gethsemani. Trappist, KY: Abbey of Gethsemani, 1946.

Gallagher, Timothy M., O.M.V. *The Discernment of Spirits: An Ignatian Guide for Everyday Living.* New York: Crossroad Publishing, 2005.

John Paul II. *Redemptoris Missio* (Mission of the Redeemer). December 7, 1990. https://www.vatican.va/content /john-paul-ii/en/encyclicals/documents/hf_jp-ii _enc_07121990_redemptoris-missio.html.

Shea, James P. *From Christendom to Apostolic Mission: Pastoral Strategies for an Apostolic Age.* Bismarck: University of Mary Press, 2020.

Stinissen, Wilfrid, O.C.D. *The Holy Spirit, Fire of Divine Love.* Translated by Sister Clare Marie, O.C.D. San Francisco: Ignatius Press, 2017.

Chapter 10

Culture

'kəlCHər | *noun* | *the customs, arts, social institutions, and achievements of a particular nation, people, or other social group.*

There's something about being in Europe that immediately makes me feel more cultured. First off, everything is older. I'll never forget walking by a pub in Vienna as I learned that it was twice as old as the U.S. Constitution. Or appreciating ancient Roman ruins that predate the lives of many of my favorite saints. Secondly, everything at least *seems* more beautiful because it's foreign and likely built before the Industrial Revolution—when there was still a happy marriage between artistry and function. For example, I'll never forget admiring the great Duomo in Milan for the first time (depicted on the front cover of this book). I also recall admiring homes along the coast of Portugal near Fatima, where our Lady appeared to three little children toward the end of the First World War.

Perhaps the most cultured I ever felt was in Paris, where I spent a long weekend fifteen years ago. I didn't know the language, and I certainly didn't grasp the full scope of the city's influence on human history. In between crêpes and museums, I should have spent more time pondering the role of Paris as the great intellectual and artistic hub of Europe during the Middle Ages. I should have read more about its role in spearheading the Enlightenment that led to its own bloody revolution and spent more time at the Louvre admiring Leonardo da Vinci's *Mona Lisa* or Eugène Delacroix's *Liberty Leading the People*. Regardless, my most significant Parisian memory took place inside the Notre-Dame Cathedral.

I stumbled into this historic church largely because I was tired from several consecutive days of walking. In an attempt to save money, I had also been eating nothing but French croissants and peanut butter for several days. As I walked into the cathedral, my young American mind was in awe of the fact that its initial construction began in 1163. I had never been inside a building—much less a church—that old. My young Catholic heart was also falling more in love with the beauty of the universal Church every day. With all its smells and bells, Notre-Dame was a microcosm of everything I loved about being Catholic. It only deepened my awareness of the Church's inestimable contributions to world history and culture.

Inside that beautiful cathedral, I found a priest who spoke English and had the longest confession of my life. He was an older Jesuit who spent well over an hour offering me spiritual counsel, friendly banter, and absolution from my sins. Next thing I knew, he invited me over for lunch with him and his brother priests. It was my first full meal in days and the only legitimate French fare I'd ever had. There were endless supplies of local cheese, wine, breads, and meat. Though I wasn't able to articulate it at the time, it was a moment that epitomized what authentic culture is all about: leisure, beauty, community, and tradition all coming together at once. It was an unforgettable day, steeped in a Catholic culture of which I was proud to be a part. Ironically, I have no French in my blood, so the symbiosis between me and this priest had little to do with food or language and everything to do with faith.

There have been countless experiences across every season of my life that point to similar, mysterious bonds with perfect strangers. What is it about the faith that can bring people together so easily and powerfully?

As a society, we often reduce our idea of culture to cuisine, language, entertainment, or politics. Or we associate it solely with high culture, like art and literature. Many of my homesteading friends also like to point out its connection with agri*culture*. But in its most fundamental expression, culture is how we share life together and what bonds us in a common *way of life*. That's what brought me together with a French priest thousands of miles away from home when I least expected it. That's what bonds me with all my closest friends who have Christ on the throne of their hearts. That's also why *culture* is the concluding principle of this book. When we live all the other principles well, Christ becomes the integrating reality of our lives and brings us into communion with fellow pilgrims who are building Christian culture in their own spheres of influence.

Sadly, many people in today's world are averse to their own heritage. Every day, more and more attempts are made at overturning the great cultural traditions and institutions that helped shape Western civilization. Even America, with its much briefer history, is facing a crisis led by revisionist historians that seems only to inspire division and self-loathing. Many Americans believe that everything about our past is evil and that the only way forward is a progressive view of politics and culture. In the words of Pope Benedict XVI, this mindset eventually leads to a "flight from one's own heritage".[1] He observes:

> Here we notice a self-hatred in the Western world that is strange and that can be considered pathological; yes, the West is making a praiseworthy attempt to be completely open to understanding foreign values, but it no longer loves itself; from now on it sees in its own history only what is blameworthy and destructive, whereas it is no longer capable of perceiving what is great and pure.[2]

Where does this "self-hatred" originate? Is authentic culture even possible without appreciating our past and recognizing the intellectual and spiritual giants who have gone before us? No culture's history is perfect, but to discard it outright is nonsensical. G.K. Chesterton explains that "in history there is no Revolution that is not a Restoration."[3] He believes that "all the men in history who have really done anything with the future have had their eyes fixed upon the past."[4] I couldn't agree more. At this point in Church history, we need a renewed appreciation for the beauty of our heritage, particularly among young Catholics and other Christians steeped in liturgy and tradition. Before we can look forward with hope, we must love everything true, good, and beautiful about our past. Furthermore, we must know the culture in which we find ourselves and love it passionately enough to claim it for Christ.

---

[1] Benedict XVI, *Western Culture Today and Tomorrow*, trans. Michael J. Miller (San Francisco: Ignatius Press, 2019), p. 44.
[2] Ibid.
[3] G.K. Chesterton, *What's Wrong with the World* (Mineola, NY: Dover Publications, 2007), p. 22.
[4] Ibid.

In this sense, we have a great deal to learn from monasticism, "which among the great movements of history
[remains] the essential guarantor not only of cultural con-
tinuity, but above all of fundamental religious and moral
values, of man's awareness of his ultimate destiny".[5] These
words of Pope Benedict XVI remind us that monks have
always been the ones to keep books, prayers, and art from
being lost forever at critical junctures of human history. Who
will keep Christian faith and culture alive in these times?
Who will preserve and pass it along to future generations?

This need to cultivate "man's awareness of his ultimate
destiny" reminds me of a classic poem from J. R. R. Tolkien's *The Fellowship of the Ring*:

> All that is gold does not glitter,
>   Not all those who wander are lost;
> The old that is strong does not wither,
>   Deep roots are not reached by the frost.
> From the ashes a fire shall be woken,
>   A light from the shadows shall spring;
> Renewed shall be blade that was broken,
>   The crownless again shall be king.[6]

Written by Bilbo Baggins, this poem underscores the
hidden royalty of Strider, who appears to be merely a ranger
but is the rightful king of Gondor. Similarly, Christ's King-
ship is largely hidden from our culture right now, but he is
the rightful King of the Universe. He came as a baby two
thousand years ago, but he will come again in all his glory
at the end of time. Until then, he is the One revealing the
face of the Father's love and reminding us of our dignity and
ultimate destiny. As his disciples, we have a responsibility

[5] Benedict XVI, *Western Culture*, p. 22.
[6] J. R. R. Tolkien, *The Fellowship of the Ring* (London: Grafton, 1991), p. 230.

to point others to his Lordship and awake the fire of divine love from the ashes of our post-Christian culture.

What else is at stake in these troubling times? What is remiss in a culture that forsakes its heritage and eliminates Christ the King from the public square? As we probe these questions, it's important to remember that only the Lord Jesus Christ can bring out the best in humanity and empower us to evangelize Western civilization yet again. Only Christ can redeem all that is true, good, and beautiful. He is the Author of salvation, and our faithfulness to his great plan for these troubling times depends entirely upon his grace.

A SUPERTIDE MOMENT

As this book goes to print, an unprecedented 29 percent of Americans claim no religious affiliation at all, describing themselves as "atheists, agnostics or 'nothing in particular'."[7] The total fertility rate in America has fallen to 1.64 (its lowest recorded level).[8] The wound of fatherlessness is on the rise, with 30 percent of American children growing up in homes without their biological fathers.[9] While we have much to be thankful for given the overturning

[7] Gregory A. Smith, "About Three-in-Ten U.S. Adults Are Now Religiously Unaffiliated", Pew Research Center (website), December 14, 2021, https://www.pewforum.org/2021/12/14/about-three-in-ten-u-s-adults-are-now-religiously-unaffiliated/.

[8] Matt Hadro, " 'Demographic Earthquake'? U.S. Fertility Rates Fall Again to Record-Low Levels", *Catholic News Agency*, May 5, 2021, http://www.catholicnewsagency.com/news/247535/demographic-earthquake-us-fertility-rates-fall-again-to-record-low-levels.

[9] United States Census Bureau, "Census Bureau Releases New Report on Living Arrangements of Children", February 3, 2022, https://www.census.gov/newsroom/press-releases/2022/living-arrangements-of-chldren.html.

of *Roe v. Wade* last year, abortion has still taken 62 million American lives since 1973—more than 18 percent of an entire generation.[10] Additionally, there's no end to the secular indoctrination taking place in our schools or the widespread confusion of gender ideology. On top of it all, we're in the midst of a leadership crisis within the Church herself. The noise and confusion are pervasive.

Therefore, it seems that the 2019 fire at Notre-Dame Cathedral, 856 years after its initial construction began, is less prophetic and more reflective of where we are as a post-Christian culture. The humbling reality is that we haven't had a truly Christian culture in the West for generations. This fact should not fill us with despair but rather fuel us with zeal. It's long past time for the Church to direct all her energy to evangelization, which means committing all our personal energy to our own deepening conversion. There's no cultural renewal without personal renewal. There's no Christian culture without Christ, who entered history and gave us a whole new way of being *human*. That's what the principles of this book are all about: cultivating the art of being human with an apostolic mindset reminiscent of the early Church. To quote Chesterton one final time, "The Christian ideal has not been tried and found wanting. It has been found difficult; and left untried."[11] We must live these principles in pursuit of the Christian ideal of holiness and gradually point the world back to God.

No small task, right? One of the best ways to avoid getting overwhelmed is to rejoice in our littleness. It's how

<hr>

[10] Randall O'Bannon, "62,502,904 Babies Have Been Killed in Abortions since Roe v. Wade in 1973", LifeNews.com, January 18, 2021, https://www.lifenews.com/2021/01/18/62502904-babies-have-been-killed-in-abortions-since-roe-v-wade-in-1973/.

[11] Chesterton, *What's Wrong with the World*, p. 29.

astronauts react to being on the moon as they look back at Earth. It's how pilgrims describe their experience of praying at the tombs of great saints. It's how I feel whenever I'm in Eucharistic Adoration with thousands of young people at World Youth Day. When we embrace our littleness—with all our interior joys and struggles—we remember that we're a part of something so much bigger than ourselves. We never miss an opportunity to encounter God in the beauty of creation or in the beauty of others. The only danger, as Saint Augustine reminds us, is to confuse the beautiful things with Beauty itself:

> Too late have I loved you, O Beauty so ancient and so new, too late have I loved you! Behold, you were within me, while I was outside: it was there that I sought you, and, a deformed creature, rushed headlong upon these things of beauty which you have made. You were with me, but I was not with you.[12]

In any culture that is dark and despairing, Beauty is the answer. Not the beautiful things in creation but God who is the Author of Beauty and who never ceases to reveal himself to little ones. He alone will save our culture because he has first saved our souls. He alone died on the Cross to save us from the eternal punishment of sin and invites us into his own divine nature. Every single day, we have an opportunity to captivate the world rather than condemn it with this good news. In fact, there is far more openness to and hunger for the Gospel around us than we realize. We must "preach the word" and "be urgent in season and out of season, convince, rebuke, and exhort, be unfailing in patience and in teaching" (2 Tim 4:2).

---

[12] Augustine of Hippo, *The Confessions of Saint Augustine*, trans. John K Ryan (New York: Image Books, 1960), p. 254.

As a close friend always reminds me, we're living through a *supertide* moment in history, with all the brokenness of our post-Christian culture on full display. Who better than the Church to step into the breach? When everyone is faithful to his personal *mission* and lives it fervently, Christian culture begins to reclaim its rightful place in the world.

CHRIST, THE INTEGRATING PRINCIPLE

What follows is an abridged version of a talk I gave ten years ago at a conference in Nashville, only a few months after my brother had passed away. It serves as a helpful reminder that Christ is the integrating principle of our lives and the Beautiful One who reclaims culture for the Father's greater glory. Things seemed as dark then as they are now, yet hope was strong in my heart:

> We're living in a day and age where people don't want to have logical conversations anymore. Have you noticed this? Have you ever had a logical conversation with somebody who didn't believe that life began at conception? That's just one issue, but it's indicative of how impossible it is to reason with people in today's society.
>
> There was a painting on display last night that depicted the beauty of life in the womb as it subtly but artfully pointed to the horror of abortion. It hung in the student center of a secular college in Florida for months, and there are stories upon stories of people whose hearts were broken upon seeing it. Many of them entered into dialogue with pro-lifers who would have never had a reasonable conversation about the plight of the unborn otherwise. Their hearts were stolen away by the beauty of this image, which opened them up to the gospel of life. That's what we want to be about. We want beauty to open our heart and leave us aching for the truth that is inseparable from it.

However, in the depths of every human heart, there is light and darkness. There is desire for good and inclination to evil. The prophet Jeremiah writes, "The heart is deceitful above all things, and desperately corrupt; who can understand it?" (Jer 17:9). The human heart is easily deceived because of the fall of Adam and Eve. Every one of us knows that we're made for glory, and yet Original Sin attempts to achieve that glory apart from God, to become like God without God. And so we settle for counterfeit love. We settle for counterfeit truth, beauty, and goodness.

In Pope John Paul II's Theology of the Body, we learn about the "original shame" that cast doubt in man's heart about the deepest meaning of the gift of love. Man turns his back on God, and yet we're all made to receive his manifold grace. It's a free gift. It cannot be earned. How quickly we forget that we, too, are a gift meant to be given away. Whether it's to our spouse or to the Church as priests and religious, we are all called to be gift. And so it makes sense that the deepest wound caused by Original Sin is to forget that gift and to reject God's love.

Early on in his encyclical *Deus Caritas Est*, Pope Benedict XVI reminds us to place all our trust in God who is the source and summit of our noblest desires. Even though our hearts are fickle, we can rest in the knowledge that "being Christian is not the result of an ethical choice or a lofty idea, but the encounter with an event, a person, which gives life a new horizon and a decisive direction."[13] In other words, our hope is in the God with a human face. Our hope is in Jesus Christ.

Thanks be to God, we're not alone in our faith. That's what this conference is all about: knowing we're not alone in our noble aspirations nor our weak failings. We're all broken but beautiful in the Lord's eyes. In each and every

[13] Benedict XVI, *The Encyclicals of Benedict XVI* (London: Catholic Truth Society, 2013), p. 7.

one of us, there's light and darkness. And yet, the God with a human face, Jesus Christ, dared to become flesh and dwell among us. He stepped into the mess of our humanity, and that changed *absolutely everything*. Jesus Christ is the One who reveals God as Father. He is the One who "fully reveals man to man himself".[14]

So, what does it means to be human? What does it mean to be fully alive? Christ is the One who makes our "supreme calling clear", which is nothing short of divine life with the Father.[15] He's the One we must come to know in order to know ourselves. Only in him can we know and fulfill our deepest desires.

What is true of the human soul is true of human culture. The more human we are, the more like Christ we become. He is not only the source and summit of man's desires; He's also the source and summit of all authentic culture. For our culture to be Christian yet again, Christ must be the One who integrates our traditions, arts, and institutions. He must be the convergence point for our attitudes, behaviors, and laws. Most importantly, he must be the origin and pinnacle of our *way of life*. While the ten principles of this book are entry points for beauty to pierce our hearts, they ultimately lead us to the truth who is a Person named Jesus Christ. If we want him to be the integrating principle of our culture, he must first be the integrating principle of our lives. He is the Beautiful One who will bring about our own deepening conversion and empower us to evangelize the world yet again.

---

[14] Second Vatican Council, Pastoral Constitution on the Church in the Modern Word *Gaudium et Spes* (December 7, 1965), no. 22, https://www.vatican.va/archive/hist_councils/ii_vatican_council/documents/vat-ii_cons_19651207_gaudium-et-spes_en.html.

[15] Ibid.

It's also worth noting that Christ is the One who invites us into the greatest culture of all, where life is shared perfectly in common in the Trinity. God—who is Father, Son, and Holy Spirit—is a perfect communion of Love. All authentic culture finds its foundation and perfection in him.

IN THE ARENA

Where do we go from here? We must live these principles with hope and fervor, especially when the stakes are as high and the times are as dark as ours. We must give the world a glimpse of the Kingdom of God by placing Christ on the throne of our hearts and ultimately of our families, communities, and culture. We must get into the arena of God's love and stay there.

Imagine that it's April 23, 1910. We're back in Paris, France, hearing a speech from former U.S. president Theodore Roosevelt at one of the oldest universities in the world. The speech is entitled "Citizenship in a Republic", delivered soon after Roosevelt had finished a year-long hunting expedition in Central Africa. At one point, he offers an impassioned criticism against cynics who look down at men trying to make the world a better place. Then, he delivers one of the great inspirational messages of modern times, since quoted by everyone from Nelson Mandela to Miley Cyrus:

> It is not the critic who counts; not the man who points out how the strong man stumbles, or where the doer of deeds could have done them better. The credit belongs to the man who is actually in the arena, whose face is marred

by dust and sweat and blood; who strives valiantly; who errs, who comes short again and again, because there is no effort without error and shortcoming; but who does actually strive to do the deeds; who knows the great enthusiasms, the great devotions; who spends himself in a worthy cause; who at the best knows in the end the triumph of high achievement, and who at the worst, if he fails, at least fails while daring greatly, so that his place shall never be with those cold and timid souls who neither know victory nor defeat.[16]

For many of us, our faces are marred by dust and sweat and blood. Our culture has left us confused and tired. Life has been full of tragedy and triumph. At times, we've been pushed to our limit. Perhaps in our exhaustion we've forgotten the blessing of it all. Unlike some generations, we're aware of the growing hostility toward Christianity and have an opportunity to step into the fight and *strive valiantly* for all that is true, good, and beautiful. By reading through these principles and applying them to our lives, we're already daring greatly as we cultivate the art of being human and pursue the heights of holiness. This book exists for no other reason than to empower us to live the fullness of our humanity in imitation of Christ himself. Our culture is sick and dying because there aren't enough saints living among us. Together, we must become those saints.

Through every season of your life, God invites you into ever-greater intimacy with himself. Wherever you find yourself right now, full of "great enthusiasms" or simply exhausted by the realities of life, ask God for the courage

[16] Theodore Roosevelt, "Address at the Sorbonne in Paris, France: 'Citizenship in a Republic'", April 23, 1910, American Presidency Project (website), comp. John Woolley and Gerhard Peters, https://www.presidency.ucsb.edu/documents/address-the-sorbonne-paris-france-citizenship-republic.

and willingness to get into the arena of his love. Look for every opportunity to know "at the best ... the triumph of high achievement" and "at the worst ... fail[ure] while daring greatly".[17] It's crucial that we step into the existential void and rouse our culture of noise from its sleep. The eternal salvation of souls depends on it. God forbid we miss this once-in-a-generation opportunity to show the world what it means to be human and storm heaven with an army of souls in our wake.

Indeed, we were made for such a time as this. *If not now, then when? If not us, then who?*

GETTING PRACTICAL

- Host an evening of culture in your home with family and friends. Make food, debate philosophy, read a play out loud, or watch a classic film together. Get inspired by the culture you already have at your fingertips.
- Visit a part of your city or country that has a totally different culture from yours. Admire all that is true, good, and beautiful while noticing what makes it similar to and distinct from yours.
- Look for small ways to bring Christ to the forefront of your family, business, or school. Over time, look for ways to make him their integrating principle.
- Work the land entrusted to you, even if it's as simple as growing a garden in your backyard. Reconnect with the beauty of God's creation right in your midst.
- As has already been suggested, read this book again with your family or a small group of friends. Build a shared way of life around these principles until Christian culture is rebuilt all around you.

[17] Ibid.

FURTHER READING

Benedict XVI. *Western Culture Today and Tomorrow*. Translated by Michael J. Miller. San Francisco: Ignatius Press, 2019.

Chaput, Charles J., O.F.M. Cap. *Strangers in a Strange Land: Living the Catholic Faith in a Post-Christian World*. New York: Henry Holt, 2017.

Senior, John. *The Restoration of Christian Culture*. Norfolk, VA: IHS Press, 2008.

Staudt, R. Jared. *Restoring Humanity: Essays on the Evangelization of Culture*. Belmont, NC: Divine Providence Press, 2020.

Wolfe, Gregory. *Beauty Will Save the World: Recovering the Human in an Ideological Age*. Wilmington, DE: Intercollegiate Studies Institute, 2014.

In a 1969 German radio broadcast, then Father Joseph Ratzinger gave the following prediction about the future of the Church:

> From the crisis of today the Church of tomorrow will emerge—a Church that has lost much. She will become small and will have to start afresh more or less from the beginning. She will no longer be able to inhabit many of the edifices she built in prosperity. As the number of her adherents diminishes, so it will lose many of her social privileges. In contrast to an earlier age, it will be seen much more as a voluntary society, entered only by free decision. As a small society, it will make much bigger demands on the initiative of her individual members.... But in all of the changes at which one might guess, the Church will find her essence afresh and with full conviction in that which was always at her center: faith in the triune God, in

Jesus Christ, the Son of God made man, in the presence
of the Spirit....

It will be hard going for the Church, for the process of
crystallization and clarification will cost her much valuable
energy. It will make her poor and cause her to become the
Church of the meek.... But when the trial of this sifting
is past, a great power will flow from a more spiritualized
and simplified Church. Men in a totally planned world
will find themselves unspeakably lonely. If they have completely lost sight of God, they will feel the whole horror
of their poverty. Then they will discover the little flock of
believers as something wholly new. They will discover it
as a hope that is meant for them, an answer for which they
have always been searching in secret.

And so it seems certain to me that the Church is facing
very hard times. The real crisis has scarcely begun. We will
have to count on terrific upheavals. But I am equally certain about what will remain at the end: not the Church of
the political cult, which is dead already, but the Church of
faith. It may well no longer be the dominant social power
to the extent that she was until recently; but it will enjoy
a fresh blossoming and be seen as man's home, where he
will find life and hope beyond death.[18]

---

[18] Cited in Tod Warner, "When Father Joseph Ratzinger Predicted the
Future of the Church", *Aleteia*, June 13, 2016, https://aleteia.org/2016/06/13
/when-cardinal-joseph-ratzinger-predicted-the-future-of-the-church/.

AFTERWORD

The story of salvation fascinates me, in all of its forms and expressions: the journey of the people of Israel out of slavery in Egypt toward their true homeland that was to be freely given to them; the warnings and rebukes issued by God through the prophets; the rise and fall of the Temple in Jerusalem; the fall of the Great City itself as its inhabitants are taken into exile; and the sense of jubilation when God brings them home again. The climax of this story is found in the Incarnation of Jesus Christ, the second Person of the Holy Trinity, who becomes flesh in our midst. He is the eternal High Priest passing through the heavens and becoming like us in all things but sin, so that we might have a high priest and advocate before the Father who is able—in every way—to sympathize with our weakness. As a high school theology teacher, adjunct professor, parish priest, and beloved son of the Father, I stand before these mysteries in silence, simply fascinated.

The beautiful thing, of course, about the Christian confession is that it holds as a central tenet the belief that through God's own revelation in the Person of Jesus Christ, made known to us through the Scriptures and Tradition, *we can come to know God*. In our cultural moment, knowing God and being in a relationship with him can seem daunting, and while many are interested in faith, they often simply don't know how or where to begin; sometimes it can all seem so complicated.

We are all familiar with the phrase "Everything I need to know I learned in kindergarten." Let me assure you that everything you need to know to be successful in the pursuit of God, and to begin living authentically the ten principles laid out for us by Jimmy Mitchell, is found at the very beginning of the story of salvation in the book of Genesis. After each moment of creation, God pauses to look upon it and, Genesis tells us, "sees that it was very good". At the end of creation, "God saw everything that he had made, and behold, it was very good" (1:31).

Remember that these words were not written by someone naive, living apart from real people with real history and real difficulties. These words were written many centuries into the story of Israel's fall and redemption, a very long journey indeed. At the conclusion of this journey, the author of Genesis is still able to affirm the goodness of creation and *the positivity of reality*.

The ten principles that have been laid out in this book help us to live a different kind of life, which includes a new way of approaching not just "the cosmos" as an abstract reality, but the daily circumstances and difficulties of life. When we hear someone say that, despite everything, reality is positive, we might react with a sense of disbelief or shock. After all, there is no shortage of evidence that might confirm the exact opposite thesis, that reality is actually ontologically negative.

For the Christian, this can't be! Reality, Father Julián Carrón tells us, is "positive because of the Mystery that dwells in it".[1] My prayer is that these ten principles will become a framework for your life, a means by which you begin to think, to pray, to choose, to live in a new way. The Christians of the present age will not fulfill their mission of responding to the culture simply by becoming more

---

[1] Julián Carrón, *Disarming Beauty: Essays on Faith, Truth, and Freedom* (Notre Dame, IN: University of Notre Dame Press, 2017), p. 201.

pious, but instead by using our humanity—our reason and will—in a fuller way, which will become for others a witness that challenges, a testimony to a life lived differently, to a life that rejoices in abundance.

Reality is good because Jesus remains present to all those who believe. Everything—even that which is most undesirable—is good simply because he remains present, just as promised. May a sincere adherence to these principles be a new means by which we might recognize this presence and begin to experience a more intentional, more free, more abundant way of life.

Rev. Ryan Adorjan, S.T.B., C.S.M.A.
Solemnity of All Saints, 2022
Naperville, Illinois

ACKNOWLEDGMENTS

This book was a long time coming and born from the fruits of many conversations, relationships, and prayers. I want to first thank Mom, Dad, and my sister, Haylee, who have been supportive of all my craziest ideas for as long as I can remember. My deepest thanks also go to the faculty of Marist School, Vanderbilt University, Pontifical College Josephinum, and Holy Apostles College and Seminary. Each of these institutions provided a space for critical thinking and intellectual leisure that laid the foundation for every idea presented in this book. Special thanks also to David Lee, Marisol Ross, Jessamyn Frain, Janaya McCallum, Tommy Killackey, Gabriel Heidbreder, and our many Love Good apprentices whose intentional way of life inspired these ten principles. I want to thank all who read various drafts of the book and helped me finalize the manuscript: Dr. Ryan Hanning, Christina Eberle, Geoff Smith, Father Ryan Adorjan, Andy and Michelle Dalbom, Angela Hamrick, and Diego Mejia. I never could have persevered to the end without their constant feedback and encouragement. I also want to thank Tony Ryan and Ignatius Press for believing in this book.

Finally, I want to thank Pope Benedict XVI, who has been my personal hero for the last fifteen years. Most importantly, I want to give glory to my Creator and Redeemer, who has been the source of all my inspiration and zeal since my first encounter with his beauty many years ago.

ABOUT THE AUTHOR

Believing deeply in the power of beauty to evangelize culture, Jimmy Mitchell's gifts of storytelling and piano-playing have brought him to every corner of the world. On top of being the founder of Love Good, he's the director of campus ministry at Jesuit High School in Tampa, Florida, which has repeatedly made national news for its growing culture of conversion. Whether he's mentoring young people in virtue or interviewing award-winning artists in his studio, Jimmy loves nothing more than helping others fall in love with God.

With his undergraduate degree from Vanderbilt University and a master's in theology from Holy Apostles College and Seminary, Jimmy has always enjoyed the cross section between faith, artistry, and entrepreneurship. Along with several artist friends, he launched Love Good in the summer of 2013 with a forty-five-city tour across America. It has since grown into a global movement of Christians committed to evangelizing the world through beauty. Learn more today at LoveGoodAcademy.com.